Living Your American Dream

Michael Marciniak

Robert D. Reed Publishers • Bandon, Oregon

Robert D. Reed Publishers
P.O. Box 1992
Bandon, OR 97411
Phone: 541-347-9882; Fax: -9883
E-mail: 4bobreed@msn.com
Website: www.rdrpublishers.com

Editor: Jessica Bryan/Robin Colucci Hoffman, GetPublishedCoach.com
Cover Designer: Nick Zelinger, NZ Graphics.com
Book Designer: Susan Leonard, RoseIslandBookworks.com

ISBN 13: 978-1-934759-81-3
ISBN 10: 1-934759-81-3

Library of Congress Control Number: 2013932496

Manufactured, Typeset, and Printed in the United States of America

Although every precaution has been taken to verify the accuracy of the information contained herein, the author and publisher assume no responsibility for any errors or omissions. No liability is assumed for damages that may result from the use of the information contained herein.

Many of the quotes in this book were found on www.famousquotes.com, and the author wishes to express his gratitude to the people quoted and to those who created and manage this website.

To my brother Bob, my inspiration.

Contents

Preface

Human existence is filled with joy and prosperity, but it's also riddled with pain, suffering, and misfortune. Many trials are unavoidable. No matter how fortunate we are, eventually each of us will face grief, illness, and death. It's a fact of life, and I accept it without question. I am puzzled, however, by the self-afflicted aspects of suffering, such as greed, addiction, alcohol and drug abuse, dysfunctional family relationships, and general unhappiness. I have always wanted to know *why*?

These issues are not just for the poor, underprivileged, and uneducated. The same issues plague successful, wealthy people. As I witnessed similar suffering among my peers, and some of it in my own life, I began to question my definition of success. Although once I measured success by how many figures I could rack up in terms of income, how much I could buy, and how important I was, I've come to realize that "having it all" is not the key to true happiness. I've learned that when you have it all, *it* actually has *you*. In other words, there's a reason they call the fancy symbols of success "trappings." To be honest, I reached a point where taking care of all the stuff I'd accumulated and the obligations I'd created had become more of a costly burden than a source of enjoyment.

I've achieved every outer symbol of success and what some call the "American Dream." I've made millions and owned fabulous homes, boats, and other "toys." I have a beautiful wife and two fantastic children. Yet, happiness eluded me for years, so I set out on an inquiry. I was determined to understand why I was so unhappy, even with all the blessings in my life, and how I could create positive change.

Through trial and error, and reading and listening, I discovered some simple principles and applied them to my own life. In this way, I found abundant enjoyment. True wealth is having more than you need, but not more than you can handle. True success is to be happy with who you are and what you have, right now. It means finding the balance between ambition and acceptance, desire and contentment, and freedom and consistency.

These techniques are simple, but not easy. By choosing this book, you have taken the first step toward your own American Dream. I hope you discover, as I did, that your choices and thoughts are within your control; your abilities are boundless; you are better off when you pick and choose your priorities; less is best; and to create sustainable happiness you need to become disciplined in key areas of your life.

I would like to thank my wife Nancy for her never-ending support and love during the good and the bad times. We have only become stronger and more united. Thank you also to Mikey and Natalie, my children, for being so terrific. While I was writing this book, I lost my father Gene, and my dog Lucky to illness. I love and miss them both. My father taught me character, values, and courage, and he was a huge support. I'm also grateful to Lois, my mother, for teaching me compassion and how to love and care for others.

I also offer my appreciation to Robin Hoffman, my writing coach, for her sharp pencil, wit, and patience. Thank you for believing in me.

Finally, to Jessica Bryan, my editor—whose experience and ability to bring thoughts and words to life is only matched by her charm, friendliness, and kindness—thank you for sharing your gift.

Now go ahead and read on. Visit my website at www.michaelmarciniak.com and give me your feedback. I am proud to be with you on the balanced, happy, and prosperous path of life.

Michael Marciniak
Bradenton, Florida
2013

CHAPTER ONE

America is Still the Land of Opportunity

America is a land of opportunity
and don't ever forget it.

~ Will Rogers, Humorist, Social Commentator, and Actor.

Before you set out to recover your American Dream, first let's take a look at how and why this famous phrase emerged. James Truslow Adams coined the term "American Dream" in his 1931 book *The Epic of America*. He wanted to call the book "The American Dream" but his publishers objected. Adams defined the American Dream as:

. . .that dream of a land in which life should be better and richer and fuller for everyone, with opportunity for each according to ability or achievement. It is a difficult dream for the European upper classes to interpret adequately, and too many of us ourselves have grown weary and mistrustful of it. It is not a dream of motorcars and high wages merely, but a dream of a social order in which each man and each woman shall be able to attain to the fullest stature of which they are capable. And be recognized by others for what they are, regardless of the fortuitous circumstances of birth or position.

Since Adams put down these thoughts nearly 80 years ago, many millions of people have taken on the challenge and achieved "the dream." Over the past 80 years, the American Dream has become more accessible to all Americans because of advances in women's rights as well as the passage of the Civil Rights Act. But if we look closely at Adams's words, we can see clearly how a shift in values in recent years has created a distorted view of the American Dream, and this shift has led many people toward sloth and greed rather than ingenuity and ambition.

As written in the quote given above, Adams didn't describe a social order in which each man and woman should be able to attain the fullest stature of *what* they can *borrow*, but rather "[that] of which they are *capable*." Adams describes a land where people have the opportunity to live a fuller and richer life based upon their *ability*, not their credit score.

The shift in values from striving for the best you can achieve to borrowing so you can buy better stuff than your neighbor has left us with a devastating financial crisis, a stressed-out citizenry, huge unemployment and divorce rates, and a seemingly insurmountable mountain of debt, both individually and as a nation.

In the simplest terms, to recover your American Dream requires a return to the initial intent Adams wrote about, which was, interestingly, at the height of America's last major financial breakdown, The Great Depression.

This means that everyone has the right to:

- Do the best they can with what they have

- Develop their skills

- Provide value to others

- Reap rewards to the extent that honest efforts, skills, and ingenuity allow

The problems facing many Americans have been self-inflicted, not brought on by an outside uncontrollable force. Overindulgence, greed, or a lack of common sense has manifested itself in the results we now see, but the system is not doomed.

The entrepreneurial spirit in this country is alive and well. Small, privately held businesses employ over two-thirds of the workforce, and every year creative people amass extraordinary wealth through their ingenuity and follow through. I believe that a return to the original values of the American Dream is imminent, if not already in motion.

Look at the young billionaire Mark Zuckerberg, who founded Facebook. He built an empire and mind-boggling wealth in a short period of time by creating a revolutionary platform for social connection and communication, yet he lives a simple life in a small house. He is more focused on the value he can create and staying in the game than he is on what he can buy. Mark Zuckerberg is living his American Dream.

The mood is always sober at the economic bottom. America still has a tremendous entrepreneurial culture and "can-do" attitude. We will get through the current crisis, just as we have done many times before. The Great Depression was a difficult time, but more millionaires arose out of that time period than any previous era, and the same is possible today. Our diverse and open society lends itself to problem solving and creativity. Yes, many of our lost manufacturing jobs might never return, but new positions in technology, research, bioengineering, and other high-tech businesses are emerging.

As Americans, it's time for us to refocus, pay off our debts, invest more and consume less, get our own house in order, and call upon our government to do the same.

We each need to do our part. Time and time again, I hear people say, "Everyone else is taking advantage of the system, so I might as well, too." This nonsensical thinking has to stop. Only you can resolve these problems through self-reflection, a change in attitude, and a willingness to admit that *you* are the source of your own difficulties. I've been through it. Initially, it may sting a bit, but the only way to recover your American Dream is to take responsibility for where you are in the present. Blaming, complaining, and justifying repel abundance and joy.

The Reversal

The great American Ponzi scheme we've been living has come with a price, the full amount of which is still unknown. The average American has four credit cards, and

MSN.com reported on February 14, 2007 that 14 percent of Americans hold more than 10 credit cards.

In 2001, the Census Bureau said nearly 40 percent of all residential properties in the U.S. were owned free and clear. However, an *MSNBC.com* study dated December 5, 2008 revealed the number had dropped to about 30 percent, and a record one in 10 American homeowners was at least one month behind on their mortgage payments or in foreclosure. The numbers have continued to deteriorate and unemployment remains high. It will be interesting to see what future Census reports have to say about home ownership.

The American Ponzi scheme created vast amounts of wealth for certain individuals. However, strengths that are extended always become weaknesses. Consequently, we are now dealing with the hangover of debt, the housing morass, unemployment, and record deficits. The unintended consequences of obesity, relationship failures, and a decline in values are also related to a system that glorifies consumption and instant gratification, and deemphasizes work, commitment, and savings.

There is a saying on Wall Street that says, "It's never different this time." Reading Adams' words, written at the height of the Great Depression, opened my eyes. It made me realize that we have been here before. Adams wrote: "The freedom now desired by many is not freedom to do and dare but freedom from care and worry."

Sound familiar? Lessons learned are soon forgotten, and history is bound to repeat itself, but it doesn't mean *you* have to keep repeating the same mistakes.

Adams goes on to write, "The greatest discovery of my generation is that man can alter his life simply by altering his attitude of mind. There are obviously two educations. One should teach us how to make a living and the other how to live." It's amazing how the truth in these words rings as clearly today as if they were written yesterday.

You have the power and ability to set your own course. You *can* recreate yourself and redefine your American Dream, and then take action to manifest an improved life for yourself and the people you care about.

What is Your American Dream?

What is *your* definition of the American Dream? Is it realistic? Does it include fitness (health), family, friends, faith, and fun, as well as financial goals? Does it take into account what you need to feel happy and fulfilled? To me, the American Dream is having the freedom to do whatever I want, whenever I want, in accordance with the laws of God and man. It's about maintaining high standards in your professional and private life. Dream big and live within your means. You can't necessarily have and do everything you want, but through patience, perseverance, and hard work much is possible and attainable.

My American Dream is to provide wealth and happiness for my family and the charities I choose to support. It is about leaving my community, family, and future generations with more than I had and making the world a better place. The American Dream is about enjoying—and never taking for granted—the freedoms of speech, religious expression, and the free market society that so many have died to protect. Most of all, it's about enjoying relationships and being part of a culture that shares a common set of core values.

The American Dream is about living rich and abundant in health, love, and wealth. It includes making peace with the life you have, enjoying the things you can comfortably afford, and realizing that having a loving family, a set of core values, and good health are the keys to lasting happiness. You *can* find happiness in any circumstance. If you think something needs to happen "out there" so you can be happy inside, you never will be happy!

This country was built on creating a higher standard of living for future generations. Up to now, it's been assumed that a higher standard of living means accumulating more "stuff." The unanswered question is: Have we borrowed so much from future generations in order to live beyond what's reasonable that we have created a lower standard of living for our children and grandchildren?

As one of the 76 million "baby boomers," the generation born between 1945 and 1964, I realize the influence we've had on our nation. From Vietnam War protests and "free love" to muscle cars, health clubs, and Viagra®, boomers have influenced politics, corporations, and social behavior. Unfortunately, much of our behavior as a generation has been self-indulgent and shortsighted. Need exploded into greed, and necessity twisted into entitlement. This 50-year trend has hit its apex, and now we are swinging back, questioning our actions and our priorities. We are taking a new look outward to include society as a whole in our equation and asking ourselves: *Is what's good for me also good for society?*

There is an awakening some call *minimalism*, which means getting rid of unnecessary possessions in order to create a simpler, higher quality of life. Early baby boomers are now entering their Golden Age and beginning to get back to basics. They no longer want the headaches or costs associated with multiple homes and toys. They are beginning to realize that the incremental expenses and time associated with maintaining their possessions outweighs the marginal enjoyment the possessions bring. Consequently, many boomers are focused more on health, family, and creating a sense of inner calm than seeking happiness in material possessions.

Why buy a second or third home when you can go online and rent anything you want for as long as you want anywhere in the world? My family spends two weeks each year in the Florida Keys to trap lobster and dive. We recently rented a luxurious home on the ocean for two weeks. It slept eight and had every amenity imaginable, including a pool, dock, master bedroom with bath, and granite countertops. For $5,000, we enjoyed our stay, dropped the keys off with the rental agent, and never had to deal with the problems of hurricanes, taxes, insurance, and home maintenance. The days of wanting to buy and hold, or rent property out for income—with the hope of selling later for double the price— are over. If a home cost $2 million dollars to build, what is the purpose and opportunity in having your capital tied up? Include the annual operating costs of taxes, insurance, pool care, pest control, and utilities, and ask yourself: *Who needs it?*

I read an e-mail written by John Reese, a young dot-com millionaire who not long ago sold or gave away nearly every-thing he owned, including his six-bedroom home, Lamborghini, Ferrari and BMW, an expensive wardrobe, and various other such grown-up luxuries. He kept his money and investments, as well as a valuable collection of dot-com businesses. He downsized in order to have less clutter in his life and his mind, so he could put more energy into developing new ventures. I know other people who have given up large prestigious positions to gain more family time and a higher quality of life. I'm one of those individuals.

Minimalism takes all forms. John Reese's experiment was extreme, but I applaud his guts and ability to act. If every American exhibited some form of minimalistic behavior, we could still live in the most prosperous nation on the globe and have a lot less stress. My own part in this trend will not bring tears to anyone's eyes, although Nancy and I have reduced our expenses about 40 percent per year just by getting rid of stuff and downsizing. We've scrapped the idea of having a ski house; we just rent on the days we want to ski. We have eliminated needless helpers around the home, fancy dinners, outings, and shopping sprees. Our standard of living has not diminished one bit, and we feel at ease, which is the point.

Spending less money and saving more is great, but the real benefit is that getting rid of excess makes day-to-day life less complicated and frees up mental space.

Think of your brain as a computer. How much storage space do you have? With the internet, cell phones, texting, and Blackberries®, we are always on call and quickly running out of mental capacity. You cannot be relaxed or creative in this mode. Free up space in your mind, and you will be healthier and happier. My good friend John Mayo said (quoting his father), "The more you own, the more it owns you!" To rid yourself of unnecessary burdens is a big step toward the promise of *liberty* our forefathers intended.

A renewed American Dream is also about taking personal responsibility for everything you create. I believe the focus needs to shift from consumption to investment, from "practice marriages" to commitment, from funding self-serving, short-term "pork" projects to a greater commitment to educating our children and retraining our workforce so we can compete in the global marketplace. A return to long-term values will increase trust, cooperation, and accountability. This is not a complete list; however, it's the starting point to bring about a tranquil, productive, and happier life. To work for the sake of self-respect and the inherent emotional, social, and educational rewards—not just economic rewards—is one of the great opportunities of the American Dream, and it's available to all of us under any conditions.

A Brief History Lesson

I want to change your view of our great land. The United States of America began as an independent nation with the signing of The Declaration of Independence on July 4, 1776. We are still a very young nation. It's human nature to yearn for the "good ol' days," which indicates we think our best experiences are behind us. I believe the best is yet to come. Let's examine some facts and see if you agree.

When we look back at those good ol' days, a different story emerges. America has had its share of boom-to-bust periods, wars, and other crises. Since 1900, we have had World War I, the Great Depression, World War II, the Korean War, the Cold War, Viet Nam, OPEC, Sputnik, the Cuban Missile Crisis, Watergate, Kent State, the crash of October 19, 1987, Long-Term Capital Management, 9-11, the Iraq and Afghanistan Wars, and the stock market and housing crashes of 2008. These events can hardly be considered the good ol' days. Yet, look at how prosperous we have become despite these events. In fact, great periods of prosperity have either preceded or followed tough times.

We seem to be going through a period of nostalgia, and everyone seems to think yesterday was better than today. I don't think it was, and I would advise you not to wait ten years before admitting today was great. If you're hung up on nostalgia, pretend today is yesterday and just go out and have one hell of a time.

~ Art Buchwald, American humorist best known for his syndicated newspaper column

Today, we are dealing with innumerable events that will lead to greater prosperity, longevity, and quality of life. Energy independence is just around the corner. Medical breakthroughs for chronic diseases such as cancer and heart disease are closer than ever before. New technologies spring up yearly. Just look at your cell phone and your ability to use the Internet. Yet, we don't feel progress on a daily basis. Why? I believe we are working off the excesses of our last prosperous period. I also believe three big components: global production capacity, mortality and birthrates, and the baby boomers are having an impact.

Global Production

After World War II, most of the world's production capacity was destroyed. Approximately 55 million lives were lost, and about 10 percent of the casualties were Americans. This was a tragic event. America was blessed from the perspective that the war was fought on foreign soil. Other than the casualties at Pearl Harbor, America was spared having to fight the battles on her own soil.

England, Europe, Russia, and Japan were not so lucky. America, having its factories intact, was busy rebuilding the production facilities of other countries. America provided goods and services to the world, which produced wealth and led to the baby boom generation. Labor in the United States was in scarce supply. Labor benefited as wages were bid up. When wages began getting too high, entitlements were then bid up to avoid strikes and compete for skilled workers.

International trade began to blossom. Production capacity from developed countries as well as emerging countries was ramped up. The middle-class dream was sought around the globe. Countries such as Germany, Japan, Russia, and China became highly competitive. In the 1980s, Japan was thought to become the dominant global producer of goods, and now it's China.

India, Brazil, Viet Nam, and other countries are also in the mix and vying for a share of the consumer's wallet. This has forced America and other developed countries to retool, produce more goods with less labor, and become technologically more efficient. Labor pools are being downsized, benefits in terms of entitlements are being reduced, and many people are happy just to have a job even if it means they are paid less.

There has not been global destruction of production in over 60 years. This has led to a glut of production capacity around the world. We have too many things being produced. Sales are going to the lowest cost provider on merchandise available from multiple sources.

No one wants another world war to solve these issues. New technologies are springing up to compete, and corporate America is retooling, but we are only in the midst of this cycle. Just examine what is going on in the auto, steel, health, and technology industries to get a feel for these changes. America will continue to lead the world in the production of goods and services, but how we train and educate the workforce will need to be revamped. All these factors are currently being reshaped, but it takes time.

Mortality and Birthrates

Going back to 1900 again, we see that on average men had a life expectancy of around 47 years and women around 49. Today, life expectancy in the U.S. has nearly doubled. According to the National Vital Statistics Report (Vol. 58, No.1, dated August 19, 2009), men on average have a life expectancy of 75 and women have a life expectancy of approximately 80 years.

Mortality rates for children have also decreased dramatically. At the beginning of the 20th century, approximately 10 percent of all children under the age of one died. Six to nine percent of all women also died due to pregnancy-related complications. Today, the mortality rate for new infants is approximately .1 percent.

The main factors for this stunning drop in infant mortality are milk pasteurization, clean water, better nutrition, lower fertility rates, dramatically improved health care, and the availability of vaccines.

There is one more interesting fact with regards to the birthrate, which is the decline in family size since 1900. Back in the 1900s, rural families averaged six children per household; urban families averaged approximately four children. Today that number is about two.

When you combine all the data, you see healthier children and fewer of them per family, allowing women to have a career versus marrying solely for economic reasons. In 1900, women spent the majority of their life bearing and raising children. Now, the average woman spends only about 10 percent of her life in these efforts. Consequently, according to the U.S. Department of Labor, only about 5.3 million women were in the workforce in 1900 compared to over 71 million by the end of 2010.

The end result is that of the working married women, 48 percent provide half or more of household earnings and spend more than $3 trillion annually; 60 percent of them work outside the home; and since 1984, the number of women in graduate school has exceeded the number of men. Given the importance of women in the workforce, it's time for women to receive equal pay and fair treatment. These are positive trends. Women now compete for many of the jobs that once were given to men, and this is forcing the educational system to adapt. In addition, men must be retrained, educate themselves, and compete for the available jobs.

The Baby Boomers

The boomer generation continues to mold society as it ages, from early childhood to middle age, including retirement, the age many boomers are beginning to reach. Boomers have had a huge hand in the run-up in housing prices, because they purchased larger homes than previous generations, and vacation homes as well.

As of this writing, the baby boomers are in the process of downsizing. Many economists believe that spending patterns begin to change after a person hits 46 years old. We become savers rather than spenders. With 70 percent of our gross domestic produce (GDP) coming from consumer spending, this will impact future economic growth rates.

> **The conclusion is quite simple—America is *not* in decline. On the contrary, we are in the midst of substantial growth because things go in cycles, and we are in the midst of another 50-year cycle.**

The ability of women to stay fully engaged in the workforce, and baby boomers needing to work well into their sixties, seventies, and beyond, contributes to a more crowded workforce. In addition, the boomers are becoming net savers versus spenders, slowing consumption and thereby decreasing the overall growth rate of our GDP.

These are not negatives but rather a confluence of events. They are temporary in the history of America's lifespan. Ten years might seem like an eternity when you have been downsized, or you are working long hours because your employer has reduced the workforce and you must pick up the slack. These events have created an environment in which, for the time being, there are not enough jobs to support the standard of living that many Americans aspire to live. History has proven that all things evolve, and so will the downturn of the early 21st century, because it will be followed by a period of abundant jobs and more prosperity for all. This will be accomplished through innovation, education, and productivity gains through new technologies and businesses.

Now, let's turn our attention to where you—as an individual—are at this turning point in American history, and how you can begin to recreate your life and recover your American Dream.

CHAPTER TWO

You Have It All, So Now What?

Open your eyes and look within. Are you satisfied with the life you're living?

~ Bob Marley, Musician

So, you are considered successful. You worked hard to make it in your field or profession. Maybe you are a doctor, lawyer, a successful trader or salesperson, an executive, or perhaps you're running your own firm. You made a wish 20 years ago hoping to be right where you are today. You've arrived! You own a house (maybe two); you're married (or maybe divorced); and you have a couple of kids. You've got money in the bank, you wear nice clothes, and you drive a high-end car. You've got everything you thought you wanted.

Considering the circumstances, your "attitude of gratitude" should be off the charts. When you set your goals 20 years ago, you expected that by the time you achieved them you would wake up each day before the alarm clock sounded, bounce out of bed, celebrate your spouse or significant other, get dressed, and race to work so pumped up that people would envy your enthusiasm. You'd be as happy as Smilin' Bob of the Enzyte® commercials.

LIVING YOUR AMERICAN DREAM

But the truth is you get up each morning facing the realization that the content of the "book" called *you* just isn't living up to the image on the cover. You lean over the sink for a closer look in the mirror and ask yourself: *Who is this person staring back at me?* Surely, it's not the "real you," but it's been so long since you felt like yourself that you don't even remember who you are.

Yeah, you have the nice house and other material rewards, but you know you'll be paying them off forever. You'll never be able to retire. Perhaps you're badly out of shape, and you are already on medication for high cholesterol, blood pressure, and/or anxiety. Your marriage is stale, but naturally you blame your spouse for not fulfilling your needs. Shouldn't he or she know how to please you?

You don't know why, but you don't like what you see in the mirror. Despite your success, you feel alone and there's a lingering feeling deep in your gut that you just can't shake. No matter how many vacations you take or how many martinis you drink, you're just not happy, and you ask yourself: *Is this as good as it gets?* Is there a way out of this dilemma without divorcing your spouse, quitting your job, and moving to Tahiti?

Many of Life's Problems Can Be Eliminated With Money

When I was young, it bothered me that my parents were so worried about not having enough money to raise four kids. I can still remember being six years old and sitting outside crying as I listened to my mother being upset about money. I swore that someday I would earn enough to take care of my whole family. I was fortunate to grow up in a loving, close family in which relationships were cherished. From my youthful perspective, it seemed that all we lacked was money. I thought it could solve all our problems—the monthly bills, school tuition, food, fun, and the needed home or car repairs. These were the big, stressful issues for my parents.

Every week, my mom would pull out her pad and pencil, sit at the kitchen table, and make a list to keep track of the bills that needed to be paid. Sometimes, she would cry from the sheer stress of worrying. She would complain to my father that we couldn't make ends meet and ask him to put in more overtime to make a little extra. My dad never knew how much we had, and up to the day he passed he had never signed a check. He just did what he could do to bring in as much money as possible.

My mom's strategy should be a lesson for us all. She would figure how much income my father was going to earn and the amount that would be needed to pay the bills, which were always paid first. What little was left was used to buy groceries and clothes. At the end of each month, we had about $7 left! If one of us was sick or something broke, she would refigure the budget to make sure all the bills could still be paid. Perhaps we ate less or someone didn't get new shoes or clothes. She just found a way to make it work.

Things only got worse in 1968, when the union at the phone company where my dad worked went on a long strike and we were forced to go on food stamps. My father struggled to provide for his family. He painted houses, worked on a soda delivery truck, and held a job as a bartender at night. At age 11, I vowed I would never be poor, and that I would make my parents proud. I was sure of one thing—I never wanted to go through the financial difficulties my parents had gone through. I set my sights on pursuing the steady trade of carpentry.

A big turning point in my life came at age 13, when we moved out of the city to the south suburbs of Chicago. Our neighborhood was modest, yet I was fortunate to attend high school in a district with some wealthier kids. One of them, Todd Henderson, became my best friend. His father and mother, H. Harry and Sharon Henderson, were like second parents to me, and Mr. Henderson became my first mentor. They had a big home on a wooded lot, new cars and motorcycles, and they belonged to an exclusive country club.

Mr. Henderson was a successful executive. His study was filled with pictures of himself posing with past and present icons, industry leaders, and even Presidents of the United States. He exposed me to professional sporting events, plays, and fancy restaurants. I enjoyed these experiences, and I began to get the sense that carpentry wasn't likely to afford me the lifestyle I wanted to live.

The teenage mind is delusional. At 17, I believed I was 10 feet tall, bulletproof, and knew *everything*. Mr. Henderson's mentoring style was light-handed and diplomatic. He never talked down to me or told me what to do. He provided knowledge, experiences, and information, which allowed me to form my own opinion—the same opinion he would have offered if I had asked. Of course, if he had presented it as advice, I would never have listened. For example, Todd and I pictured ourselves as lifelong friends, farming together and making a fortune. Mr. Henderson called a friend in the Department of Agriculture, and in a few days we had loads of material. We soon realized that to start a farm we would need a lot of education and money, and we quickly decided farming was not in our future. This was how Mr. Henderson operated.

One day during my senior year, I waited for Todd in Mr. Henderson's 22' x 22' study, which was trimmed out in all teak. I sat quietly in front of him as he swiveled in his chair behind his big desk, behind him shelves of books, diplomas, pictures, and awards. Staring back at me were pictures of him posing with former Presidents Reagan, Bush Sr., Nixon, and Ford. It was a bit intimidating. He started asking me questions about my future plans. Mr. Henderson's questioning techniques were superb—Perry Mason certainly had nothing on him. There I sat, telling him how great it was going to be pounding nails for the rest of my life, and as I heard myself speak I began to realize carpentry might have some limitations. He sat back and listened, looked me right in the eyes in his usual relaxed way, and said, "Mike, I think carpentry would be a great hobby, but I want you to go to college."

The recession of 1974-1975 confirmed what Mr. Henderson had said, so I took his advice and charted a new course away from carpentry. I went on to get a college degree and an MBA, and then brought my "can-do" attitude to Wall Street and made a lot of money. Had I stayed with the dream of becoming a carpenter, my income would have topped out way below what I eventually achieved, and I would not have the nice house on the water, the 1,000-acre ranch near Gainesville, Florida, the fancy cars, or be able to take incredible vacations. So, having money does solve some problems.

Life is a Matter of Choices, and Every Choice has a Price

Life seemed to be going pretty much as planned until one day in 1991, when I was scheduled to make a presentation at a Shearson Lehman Brothers National Branch Managers' conference at the Waldorf Astoria. Prior to my speech, I felt exhausted and dizzy, and I had to run to my room and lie down at every break. I remember calling my wife and telling her I might need to go to the emergency room. I fought the dizziness and nausea, and barely made it through the meetings and speeches. The thought of letting someone else do my part never occurred to me. It was a huge compliment to have been chosen, and I feared not living up to the expectations of others. My greatest fear while working on Wall Street was getting fired. My friends and I would kid each other about making it to another Christmas Holiday.

The feeling that something wasn't quite right continued for about a week. I slowed down at home (but not at work) and tried to get in a bit more exercise. I chalked it up to perhaps a mild case of the flu or being a little overworked. I was a newlywed, and I had my eyes firmly fixed on the goals of landing larger offices and making more money.

Soon, everything seemed to be even better than planned, until the morning of March 9, 1993, when I picked up a copy of the *Wall Street Journal*—at the time, my wife was in labor with our first baby. One of the top stories was about how Smith Barney was set to acquire Shearson Lehman Brothers. The implications weren't clear, but the merger might mean that both my wife and I would no longer have jobs.

Nancy was in her 10th hour of labor when I had to leave her and run to the office to make some calls and have a quick sales meeting. Trust me, she was not happy about it. I just felt I had to be at the office. When I returned about three hours later, she was still in labor. Twelve hours later our son Michael was born.

Given the image I present to the world, people assume I'm one of the most self-confident people you will ever meet; however, my humble background sometimes haunts me. I feel insecure about my ability to sustain my position in life. With the merger, the three city managers for Smith Barney and Shearson Lehman Brothers knew that eventually there would be only one, and I was determined it would be me. I would be the one left standing. I began to work harder and put in longer hours, while also getting up in the middle of the night to help care for our newborn son.

The uncertainty lasted for a year—until I was told that I would be the surviving manager and lead the consolidation of three offices into one. I was thrilled and so was Nancy. The announcement was scheduled for early 1994, and I had a lot of prep work to do because the office had yet to be built out. I needed to decide the layout, where everyone would sit, and who would get the preferred offices in terms of size and view. These are big factors in the brokerage world, because appearances and prestige carry a lot of weight. The hardest part was keeping everyone in the company employed. In the mid-1990s, financial advisors could make two to three years' earnings by jumping over to another firm. Knowing this, I had to wine, dine, and schmooze all the top producers to ensure they would stay. I was pretty well set with all of them, except my top advisor.

This advisor had worked in my original office, but he was not happy with the move downtown. His thinking was his clients liked to drive right up to the office and walk in. They did not want to self-park, take an elevator, and wait in a lobby. On top of that, his office would be drastically downsized from the "palace" he'd asked the firm to build for him at the old place. Then there was the issue of file cabinets and where his assistants would sit. My greatest and final challenge was to pull it all together. We hashed it out until he was on board with the plan. When he left my office, I thought I could finally relax, but as he walked off down the hallway I began having chest pains. I told my assistant I was going to the emergency room, because I was sure I was having a heart attack.

When I got to the hospital, they told me it was merely a panic attack. While I'd heard of panic attacks, I didn't know what one was. The doctor said that my adrenaline was probably in overdrive, and when I finally relaxed my body could not turn it off. He told me to get some rest and take it easy, but instead I went back to the office.

The doctor's words did get my attention. My brother had a stroke in September 1990, and my father was recovering from his second heart attack. I started reading everything I could on brain chemistry, the fight or flight response, and diet. I also was fortunate to reach out to a friend, Art Mortell, whom I'd met back in 1986. He was a regular speaker to the new broker recruits at Shearson Lehman Brothers Training Center, and he is still a nationally recognized motivational speaker. Art told me to monitor my feelings in order to know when to modify my behavior. "Know when to throttle back," he often said, "before you get into burnout mode." He told me to listen to some CDs to relax, take short breaks during the day, and run every morning.

I took his advice, and in a few weeks time I began to feel like my old self. I thought all the stress was behind me. The offices were together, my frame of mind had improved, and I felt like I was back into growth mode. I was hoping to expand the office and eventually move on to become a Regional Director, which had been my goal since joining the firm in 1986.

I wanted to be a Regional Director for two reasons. First, the money and prestige would certainly be rewarding. But, second and more important was that I wanted to follow in the footsteps of my first professional mentor, Rudy Hlavek. At that time, Rudy was the Regional Director for North Florida, and I believed he embodied everything an executive and person should be. He was professional and well respected, and he had solid morals and values. He was the reason I had moved from Chicago to Florida. Rudy believed in me and offered me my first big opportunity. Rudy was tough, but also kind, and he had rules. He called them "Rudy's Rules."

RUDY'S RULES

The secret to life is keeping your head screwed squarely on your shoulders.

Be warm with people and cold on issues.

The best form of leadership is to lead by example.

Nothing can replace the power of a positive attitude.

Rumors are a waste of time, counter-productive, and damage your reputation.

25

Never rest on your past accomplishments.

Treat everyone with respect, regardless of title.

Live well below your means and never carry debt, and

If I have to manage the office for you, you will not be the manager.

Rudy offered so much good advice that I wrote a manual highlighting his many pearls of wisdom. I believe we have all been helped along the way. For me, Rudy epitomized everything I wanted to be as a business leader, as well as an individual.

While I was attending a meeting in Dallas, Rudy called me on the phone to ask if I was interested in becoming a Regional Director for the Chicago Region. I was thrilled. My dream job seemed to be within reach. I called my wife, who was pregnant with our second child, and she told me she did not want to move. Her reasoning was that things were going great with both our jobs; we'd just moved into a new home; Mikey was a little over a year old; and she was pregnant with another baby. The thought of moving was just too stressful for her, and, besides, she loved Florida. Everything I'd worked for seemed to evaporate, and it was upsetting. Sure, I would have to be interviewed, so it wasn't a sure thing, but to turn down this kind of offer from the firm outright was professional suicide.

I told Rudy why I could not apply for the position and went back to the meeting feeling hollow and bitter. About an hour later, I got another call from Rudy. He said the President would love to see me, have me interview for the position, and get to know him. Given what had just happened, I wasn't thinking clearly. I told him it would not be worth either his time or mine, because my wife didn't want to move. Rudy tried changing my mind but I was firm.

Moments later, sitting back in the auditorium, I had a sinking feeling. What had I just done? Why did I just say those things? Why didn't I just hop on a plane and meet the President? If I got the job, I could always decline for family reasons. But to say I didn't want to meet with him—that was probably a bad decision. In fact, I *knew* it was a very bad decision.

Natalie was born on July 31, 1994. My office was doing great, the kids were a handful, but wonderful, and Nancy's career as a financial advisor was on the upswing. My health was perfect, and we had begun saving to buy a house on the water.

Rudy was now a Divisional Director for the Midwest. I really missed having him as my supervisor. One day he called to ask if I would consider applying for the Chicago Regional position, as it had become available again. Ever the diplomat, he said, "Talk to Nancy, and if you have an interest let me know."

I was excited when I hung up the phone. The opportunity for a huge promotion making more money, getting back to my hometown, and working for my mentor was a dream come true. Rather than call Nancy right away, I waited until that evening to tell her. I would need all my sales skills once I got home.

I waited for the kids to go to bed, and then I brought up the subject. "Rudy called and asked if we would be interested going back to Chicago. The Regional Director position just became available."

There was dead silence. Twelve years of experience in sales told me I wouldn't be able to budge her. She reluctantly agreed to my doing the interview, but my heart wasn't in it. I knew that if I received the offer, I would have to turn it down. I knew enough, even then, not to pit Nancy's happiness against my career.

When I got to the interview, I felt like an imposter at my own opportunity. I knew there was no way I could accept the position even if they offered it to me, yet I couldn't afford to give the President another snub. When he asked how my wife felt about moving, I told him she was reluctant. Unfortunately, I also made an off-color remark as to how "I was not a lucky sperm and had to climb my way up." He looked over his glasses and just stared at me. I knew then it was all over. I left the interview feeling terrible, certain I would not get the offer and knowing I had sabotaged the interview rather than risk the possible embarrassment of turning it down.

For about a month, I waited nervously for a call from Rudy as to my fate. Finally, on a Saturday afternoon, I got the news I was expecting. Rudy asked me how the interview had gone, which (as every manager knows) is the way to start a conversation about bad news. Let the candidate tell you why they are not getting the job; that way it will be hard for them to argue with the verdict. Rudy said I might be ready to be the North Florida Regional Director, but not Director of the larger Chicago region. A few weeks later, they announced the new Regional Director for North Florida. He was a friend of mine. I had lost out on both promotions.

My world was shattered. Prior to the interview, Rudy and his boss told me I could have my pick of any region I wanted. Now, I had neither. I'd been passed over, and I felt embarrassed and let down. All the sacrifice seemed to be for naught. It seemed that neither the firm nor my wife recognized my hard work or supported me. I felt stuck in a position that had once appeared limitless, but now it seemed old and stale, a dead-end.

While working out with my personal trainer one morning, my heart started racing, I felt terrible and nauseated. I recognized the sensations as another anxiety attack. This time, I didn't go to the hospital. I showered, went to the office, and pushed my way through another day. When I got home, I told my wife what had happened. Her response was, "Stop thinking and try to relax. It will pass just like the times before."

But it felt different this time. I was stuck. I'd convinced myself that my career path had hit a dead-end. My dreams would have to shrink to fit this new reality, and I was not mentally ready for it. I limped through life for about a year feeling miserable and keeping my internal discord to myself, except for telling my mom and dad, Nancy, and Art Mortell. However, this time Art's pep talks and taking personal time off were no longer enough. I needed professional help.

I consulted with Jim Loehr, Ed.D. in Orlando, Florida, who conducted a battery of tests and ordered extensive blood work. All of the test results showed that I was physically healthy, so the question remained: Why was I still feeling poorly?

I started taking private Tae Kwon Do lessons. This broke up the week and gave me something to look forward to, but I still needed to get down to the real issues. Why was I afraid? What lingering issues were causing such mental anguish? Why didn't I enjoy the things I'd worked so hard to accumulate? My wife would list our blessings: the house, life in paradise, our kids, the country club, our boat, and our friends, but I was still unhappy. I had trouble sleeping. I felt jittery most of the day, and I'd lost my appetite. It was hard to have fun with the kids. I turned my analytical skills toward trying to figure out what was going on inside my head.

In 1997, our huge house on the water was under construction. It was to be my wife's dream home. I knew if she had been resistant to moving before, she would never move now. I felt this was the final "nail in the coffin" as far as my ability to move my career forward. I called our family doctor and made an appointment. He prescribed Xanax® to calm my nerves and some antidepressants. I told him I was totally against taking pills, but he talked me into it. I figured I had nothing to lose. I was taking a week off to move the family, and he had said to call him if I had a problem. I bought the drugs, even as I feared telling my wife. That evening, I took one Paxil® and fell asleep.

I woke up at about 2 a.m. feeling agitated and so weak I could hardly stand. Although suicide was never an issue, taking more pills might make it an option! I called the doctor in the morning, and he told me to keep taking them. I flushed the pills down the toilet and never saw that doctor again.

I decided to see an acupuncturist, Dr. Ruan Zhao. Two people in my office who had cancer had said great things about him. He prescribed several herbs and weekly acupuncture treatments to calm my nerves and help me sleep. Within three months, I began to feel normal again, and Dr. Zhao slowly weaned me off the herbs. I've continued monthly visits to this day as a preventive treatment, and I'd recommend Chinese medicine to anyone.

I also consulted a licensed social worker for about four months, and I'll share with you now some of the things I learned during this process:

- Lose the inner critic, that little voice in your own mind that keeps saying you have to be perfect and please everyone else, even at the cost of your own health.

- Stop playing "what if."

- When you get tired, stop working and relax for a while. No one will judge you.

- Take care of your body and physical health.

- Set your own priorities. Don't let others dictate what's really important to you and your family.

- Passion comes from learning and growing.

- There are always options for handling difficulties. You don't need to avoid your problems or succumb to doubt and fear.

- Put your problems in perspective. When you write down everything that bothers you on a piece of paper, you will realize that things aren't so bad—no one has been injured or died!

- Be present in the moment.

- Enjoy your success now. If not now, when?

- Forget about the fear of failure. You have the skills and proper preparation.

- Focus on your health and your family, because nothing else matters. When you leave work, all your energy needs to go to them.

- Over-achieving requires you to work too hard; strive to be balanced and more relaxed.

- Do more creative thinking and less worrying.

- Believe that everything you want to do will be easy, and it will be.

- Focus on what *you* want, not on what you don't want.

- Finally, read and remember the Serenity Prayer (written by Reinhold Niebuhr): "God grant me the serenity to accept the things I cannot change, the courage to change the things I can, and the wisdom to know the difference...."

I suffered for over five years from a condition that was entirely self-inflicted. It wasn't the job, the firm, a boss, or my wife. It was my own inability to confront and handle my fear of failure and fear of losing what I had. My priorities were backward. I put working nearly every waking moment for people who did not care about me above being available to my family. My entire life was about one thing: making money. I made more and more of it and kept buying more "stuff," but I was also less satisfied because I was sacrificing family, fitness, faith, friends, and having fun.

Taking Paxil® and waking up at 2 a.m. feeling like the world was about to end was the alarm I needed to begin the long process of reevaluation and getting into alignment with what truly matters and becoming authentically happy.

As challenging as that time was, it led me to reexamine my life and how I wanted to live. I have gone from poor to rich, happy to depressed, healthy to unhealthy and back again. Growing up poor, I was determined to provide for my family. I worked hard and sacrificed to achieve this goal. I wanted to be financially secure and never have to worry about money. I succeeded, but I also nearly sacrificed what I *did* have growing up, which was a loving family, my health, and inner happiness. Taking a promotion that would require a move as well as extensive travel would have meant more money but even less balance. I got honest with myself and realized it was no longer about my honorable aim of providing for my family. My ambition had become about ego gratification, and it seemed my ego would sacrifice my health, my marriage, and anything else in the way—if I let it. With this realization, I vowed I would rather quit or take a lesser role than allow my own self-destruction.

Access to happiness requires that we take responsibility for what we create. Many people are unhappy because they are caught up in a scenario of "blame, complain, and justify." As long as we continue to blame others, justify our own wrongdoings, or complain about our circumstances, we will never be happy. Failure to take responsibility means we see ourselves as victims, and victims are never happy.

My breakthrough in getting back to happiness and balance was acknowledging that the dream I was chasing was already achieved. I had it in my grasp, but I had failed to recognize it for years. I had great health, a beautiful family, a stunning home, and financial freedom. I had to get my ego in check and decide that my core happiness was more important than money. I felt liberated and happy for the first time in years.

My personal struggle has helped me coach many other people who are success-bound, but who have lost sight of the priorities that lead to happiness. Happiness is humanity's birthright. It has no social or economic prerequisite. Everyone has access to it. If you live a balanced life and stay true to your core, you will enjoy the things you have earned. You can still make a lot of money and have nice things, but with everything you buy there will be a price to be paid *and* a cost. The price is what you pay at the checkout counter. The cost is the energy it takes to earn the money for the purchase and maintain it. The cost is the sum of the *unintended consequences*, and you must be prepared to handle them.

I reclaimed my happiness when I was able to admit that I had screwed up, and that the choice was mine and mine alone. To be happy, I had to face the fact that my thoughts, words, and actions had led me to the breaking point, and that it was my choice to put success ahead of happiness. I had chosen to turn away from my core self, but I could also choose to find my way back again.

CHAPTER THREE

American Dream or Ponzi Scheme?

Have a dream, have hope, and keep fighting.

~ Lola Jones, Olympic Athlete

Stand in any grocery checkout line and look at the magazine headlines. They never change. Month after month, year after year, the American consumer is offered the latest, greatest solution to lose weight fast, make more money, and have a better sex life. Obviously, people want the information because these magazines sell millions of copies. But despite all of this expert advice, many people seem to be going in the opposite direction. Obesity continues to rise; people are struggling with their finances now more than ever; and marriages are dissolving like cotton candy on a hot humid day.

So, what happened to the American Dream and is it still achievable?

In the early days of the Republic, the goal of most people was not extravagant wealth, but rather economic independence and the opportunity for social advancement through financial gain. Benjamin Franklin's famous quote "Early to bed and early to rise, makes a man healthy, wealthy, and wise" became the mantra that symbolized America's ingenuity and work ethic.

The rise of industry marked the beginning of a decline in the American work ethic, as assembly line production and technology began to eliminate the need for a skilled labor force. As early as the 1950s, the value Americans once placed on hard work and thrift became eclipsed by a desire for status and material possessions. With this shift in consciousness, the American Dream was transformed from an inspiration to support a strong work ethic to a sense of entitlement. As Matthew Warshauer wrote in his 2003 article "Who Wants to be a Millionaire, Changing Conceptions of the American Dream:"

> The American Dream has been reduced to a quest for the almighty dollar and is marketed to the masses as a "quick fix" to get to the "good life through state lotteries, infomercials, game shows (such as *Deal or No Deal* and *Who Wants To Be a Millionaire*), and in high-profile, high-compensation lawsuits.
> (*American Studies Today Online*, www.americansc.org. uk/Online/American Dream.htm)

Many people are looking to, wishing for, and even *expecting* get-rich-quick solutions to bring them financial independence. Thus, they overlook the tradition of hard work and spending less than they earn. This type of thinking has only intensified since the 1980s, as Americans have witnessed a stock bubble *and* a real estate bubble, watching in awe and envy as a few savvy investors created extreme wealth in a very short period of time. Never mind when the bubbles went "pop," or the crashes that followed in which thousands lost it all. To most, the American dream has devolved into "get yours while you can as fast as you can, and if you can't, put it on credit."

The media has a big part in promoting the "get rich today" philosophy. Commercials and infomercials preach the idea of making instant millions, while reality proves otherwise. Serial television shows consistently portray characters living in homes and driving cars that would be way outside the reach of someone in real life with the same career. Shows such as *Lifestyles of the Rich and Famous* glamorize the lives of rich people as if all problems evaporate into the ethers when you reach a certain net worth. It's easy to get caught up in "insta-rich" thinking, but it's a fatal trap for anyone who actually wants to get rich and stay rich.

There is only one way to get rich, and that is through consistent, focused work and disciplined, smart investing. Spending may make you *look* rich, but over the long term what have you accomplished? Will being in debt and having financial problems make you happier, help your marriage, or bring you closer to retirement or financial independence? Sacrifice is not easy, but it leads to greater peace of mind and a higher quality of life.

Pay yourself first, not the credit card companies or the banks. Make it your goal to have no debt, or as little as possible.

I have known countless people who appear to be very successful. They have a big house and fancy cars, and as a result they owe more than they're worth. When you're leveraged to the hilt, even the slightest downturn in the economy or your income can trigger a chain reaction, catapulting you into bankruptcy. Save at least five percent of your earnings, and you will have at least some cushion between you and the ups and downs of volatile economic times. Save 20 percent of your earnings, and you will be able to enjoy the ride.

Invest wisely. You have worked hard for your money, and you made many sacrifices to set aside money to invest. You hope to retire comfortably, and you have a strong desire to make your money work for you. Here are some suggestions for managing money that will help you make good choices:

- Don't invest with "one-man shops" or small firms. Work with a firm that has "deep pockets" and a compliance department and legal staff to keep the brokers in check.

- If you don't understand a particular investment, don't buy it. Never be pressured into something on the basis that if you don't invest you will miss a great opportunity. Good investments are like buses—there is always another one coming.

- Never hand your money over to another person and let them handle the funds on your behalf. Keep some liquidity and control your own money; this means you will have some capital available to take advantage of a great investment opportunity.

- Avoid get-rich schemes.

- Never invest in businesses or things that are unfamiliar.

- Maximize your contributions to your 401(k) plan in order to provide for your retirement and protect your family.

- Dollar cost average into quality mutual funds or high quality stocks. In other words, set aside a certain sum of money to be invested monthly and avoid trying to time the market.

The best financial advisors are trained to help you grow your net worth over time and protect your money from the ravages of inflation and preserve wealth. They can help take the emotion out of investing and guide you through the myriad of choices. They will help protect you from bad investments and from your own emotions. A client's greed, especially when they already have wealth, is the killer. I have seen numerous wealthy clients get greedy, pull a risky move, and lose the bulk of their net worth. Be happy with the money that took years to save, and protect it through sound financial planning.

The New Capitalism: A Tenuous Ponzi Scheme

The Declaration of Independence, which was radical for its time, states, "We hold these truths to be self-evident, that all men are created equal, that they are endowed by their Creator with certain unalienable Rights, [and] that among these are Life, Liberty and the Pursuit of Happiness." These values are the foundation of the American Dream, and they have inspired millions over the past two and a half centuries. The original statement was the right to the pursuit of property, but Benjamin Franklin suggested replacing this idea with happiness. However, if you look at social behavior over recent years, the quest for property has superseded the desire for liberty, and in many cases, even life. But what happened to the pursuit of happiness? Good question.

The American economy has become the most giant Ponzi scheme in the history of the world. According to Wikipedia, a Ponzi scheme is "a fraudulent investment operation that pays returns to separate investors from their own money or money paid by subsequent investors." Our economy is driven by debt and consumption. In other words, consumers use money they don't have to buy goods that the store added to its inventory with borrowed money. More borrowed money is used to make the payments back to the credit card companies, which borrowed the money they lent to the consumer from bigger banks or the Federal Reserve. Once the consumer can no longer pay on their debts, the big banks go to the federal government for a bailout that is paid for with—you've got it—money borrowed from China.

As a society, we are raising generation after generation of irresponsible spenders when we could be training savvy capitalists. I have not seen one class in high school or college in this country that teaches personal financial responsibility. So why doesn't our great nation have an interest in teaching these useful skills, even if it means less time spent memorizing the elements of the periodic table or learning the theories of macroeconomics? The sad fact is that the stock prices of banks, credit card companies, and mortgage companies only go higher with greater earnings, and they only have higher earnings when there is a growing consumer base willing to take on more debt. With more debt, the consumer pays higher interest, which gives the banks more money, and this gives the consumer the ability to spend more money on items they don't need—usually items made overseas, which often sends money to China and other nations with which we have a trade deficit. The purchases are then taxed by your local, state, and federal government, filling their coffers so they can bail out the banks when consumers default under overwhelming debt, and so the cycle keeps on going.

The banking crisis of 2008 illustrates this scenario perfectly. How did we get into that mess? Numerous experts trace the causes back to the federal government with the advent of the Community Reinvestment Act and the leveraging of Freddie Mac and Fannie Mae. Politicians pressured banking institutions to irresponsibly lend to people who could not afford to borrow the funds in the first place. Our city, state, and federal governments were complicit, because there were no regulations in place to educate the consumer or protect them.

Despite government promises to add regulations and consumer protection, the only solution lies with the individual. Regulations put on banks with regard to derivative exposure and proprietary trading will not stop you from maximizing your credit card debt. Nor will it stop you from buying too big of a house. If you really want it, you'll find a way to finance it. All of us can stop this cycle by living within our means and reducing the amount of debt we personally assume.

Focus on Values, not Consumption

People who work on Wall Street live to get paid one day per year. That's the day the bonuses hit, which is usually in late January. Managers, investment bankers, sales support, and other employees get a small salary, but 70 to 90 percent or more of their earnings come in the form of a bonus. For me, it was the happiest day of the year—and the saddest day of the year. Happy in that I was paid. Sad because I would have to wait another 364 days to get paid a large amount again. If you spend without the discipline of saving and living within your means, it's pretty easy to burn through 364 days of income in just a few months. Countless people ruin their finances by violating the basic commandment: *Never have debt and live within your means.* You never know how secure your job is; you never know if you will get ill; and what if your income flat lines or drops?

Plan for the worst and hope for the best.
Be disciplined in your saving and spending,
and your life will be much easier.

When I was supervising a financial office, the average advisor was earning in excess of $200,000 per year. Some earned more than $1 million. I always found it interesting how certain individuals could make that income for 10 or even 20 years and not have any money saved! To make matters worse, some of them would trade their accounts, get into investments that failed, or do things that were unethical, just to maintain the standard of living they thought would bring them happiness. Bernie Madoff is the ultimate example of playing on people's greed to feed his own, bilking thousands of investors out of billions of dollars—and these were smart, successful people just like you and me.

As the world's largest consumer nation, the success of our economy depends upon everyone buying more stuff.

Seventy percent of our gross domestic product (GDP) is consumer spending. We all want to enjoy life's luxuries and ensure that America stays strong, but we need to do it responsibly and within our means. Unfortunately, as your income goes up, your monthly expenses also go up. Then you have to work harder to keep the Ponzi scheme going, because you not only need to pay for what you have, but in some perverse way you think you will be happier when you buy even more. Therefore, as the years go by, your net worth goals keep getting adjusted upward to match your perceived "necessary" standard of living. Your time horizon for financial independence and enjoyment of these hard-earned dollars is also pushed farther and farther out into the future, and for many that future never comes.

I had a friend whose goal was a net worth of $5 million. Once he reached his goal at around age 60, he felt his goal should be $6 million. Over the course of the next eight years, he kept increasing his net worth goal until it reached $8 million, but then he died at age 68! How sad that he never enjoyed the fruits of his labor. What was his thought process? Why couldn't he just sit back and enjoy what took him more than 40 years to build?

Even after my friend died, I was stuck on the same track. But don't get me wrong; striving to reach higher goals is a good thing. We should all aspire to do better and raise the bar for personal growth. But I had stopped enjoying what I was doing, and I didn't *need* to do it anymore, so why did I persist? Failure to realize that "enough money" is a moving target, and having an attitude of "I'll be happy when...." only puts off the happiness you have access to right now and makes you lose sight of what is truly important.

Having "Enough" is a Moving Target

Think about your own financial goals. How much is enough? If you go back 10, 20, or even 30 years, how has it changed? How much have you adjusted your goal as the result of inflation or the cost of living? How much has it changed because of what you think you need to be happy? What will it look like in the next 10 years? How about 20 years, or longer? The key is to set up proper expectations and goals. What do you want to accomplish in life (besides making money) while you still have good health? Certainly, an experienced financial advisor can assist you in setting goals and making a plan that works for you. Will you live your life for one day that may never come, or learn to enjoy life in the present and revel in the journey and your hard work along the way? The choice is yours.

We are always getting ready to live, but never living.
~ Ralph Waldo Emerson, American Essayist and Poet

Be Careful What You Ask For

My whole life, I worked tirelessly so I could retire when I was 50 years old. Well, I did it at 51! Boredom set in almost instantly, and I felt almost as much stress as when I was working so hard. I know what you're probably thinking: *I'll switch with you!* I said the same thing looking from the outside in. You need to have structure and purpose in your life in order to avoid boredom. I don't want to work from 7 a.m. to 7 p.m. ever again, but I also don't want to go 24/7 with nothing to do, no one to do it with, and no value to bring to the world. The key is doing something you enjoy so it doesn't feel like work, and if you must have a job, enjoy it.

The Working Rich

You may have dreamt of retirement ever since your first day of work, but times are changing, and now people are more interested in achieving personal fulfillment than living a sedentary life of leisure. I believe that no one would retire if their job allowed them to be fully engaged and provided a sense of self worth, accomplishment, and balance. Humans need something to do. Whether this means engaging in sports, traveling, reading, or exercising, if you can make money at something you enjoy, would you call it work?

I have known many people who retired early only to discover that they can play golf and go fishing only so much before they start looking for something more worthwhile to do. People who work into their later years remain mentally sharp and aware longer. They feel more alive and a greater sense of belonging, contribution, and usefulness. Staying engaged with friends supports healthy self-esteem and ensures better health. Before you retire or quit your job, research all your options. Many companies have flexible hours and some allow employees to work remotely, or perhaps it's time to start your own business or go work for a charity with a mission that inspires you. I have met countless people in their eighties, and some in their nineties, who are still working in some capacity. When I ask them what accounts for their health and longevity, they always credit staying active.

Maybe it's not retirement you want, but a change of pace—a forgotten dream you wish to pursue, a part of you that got left behind and needs to be reclaimed and expressed. The key is to enjoy your life. More than likely, this includes being active and feeling useful.

CHAPTER FOUR

Recreate Your Life and Recover Your American Dream

Unless you're ready to think, feel, and act in different ways than you've done prior to now, you'll continue to live the life that you're living with the results you've been getting.

~ James Arthur Ray, Author of *Harmonic Wealth*, a *New York Times* Bestseller

When I spoke with someone about what I was writing, he responded that he didn't want to be anyone else in the whole world. "I have just enough—a nice home, plenty to eat, and my basic needs are met with sufficient income left over to save for retirement." His gratitude was palpable. He's living his American Dream! He's making far less than some, but he is richer than most. Where do you stand with regard to your expectations and needs? What do you need to truly be happy? How sure are you that it's the right choice?

At times, we begin to feel stagnant, stale, and stuck. You're not *un*happy; you've just lost the spark. The excitement is gone. How do you get it back? How do you stay engaged? To recover your American Dream, you will most likely need to recreate your life, which means staying engaged. It's as much about self-improvement and getting to the next level as it is about being happy and content where you are.

Professional athletes recreate themselves by getting in better shape, changing their training patterns, and seeking out new coaches. Sometimes, subtle shifts can change a person's attitude and mind-set, resulting in more competence, higher efficiency, and a stronger mind and body.

A change in attitude creates excitement in life, work, and relationships.

Let's go back in time to learn how you can be more inspired and excited about your present life. Close your eyes and remember when you were a child. How excited and happy you were when you won a game or trophy, got invited to a dance, received a diploma or driver's license, got your first car, or perhaps your first kiss? It was all so new, a rite of passage, a process of gaining independence or entering adulthood. How many times have you caught yourself saying, "I can't wait until. . . .," and then before you could blink, you'd arrived? You graduated. You started working, got married, and had kids. Typically, at the moment we achieve one thing we begin to wish for the next. As soon as we get a job, we begin wishing for a vacation, a promotion, a different job, or retirement.

Less is Best

For nearly 250 years, the possibility of health, wealth, and happiness has inspired entire generations and remains the

American ideal. We live in a society of unlimited potential. Everyone has access to achieve his or her heart's desire. The reality that our forefathers understood, yet many overlook today, is that life is tough, and it takes tremendous discipline to achieve even the simplest pleasures and rewards.

One paradox in life is that the more we have, the more we want—and the less satisfied we are with the things we get. I have learned that less is best, but I had to get more to want less! Let me explain. Growing up poor, if and when I received a few gifts for my birthday or a holiday, I was in heaven. Likewise, when I began working, I felt great satisfaction in buying my first suit, a car, and new furniture. I didn't have much, so the things I bought were easy to maintain. I did not realize it at the time, but the true joy was the challenge and the journey.

As I became more successful, I bought more things: boats, jet skis, clothes, sporting goods, and other toys. Later, I realized that I had to take care of these objects, and this pressed me for what little free time I had. My possessions became more of a nuisance than a joy. Caring for the things I bought also wasted money and gave me little personal satisfaction. The easier it was to attain, the more quickly I got bored with each new purchase. If you don't believe me, look at celebrities who have multiple homes, boats, and cars. Are their marriages lasting longer? Do they use fewer drugs, drink less alcohol, and have more happiness? Consider the examples set by Michael Jackson, Marilyn Monroe, and Elvis Presley.

People need to love and be loved. Everything else is baggage, and, in many cases, a poor substitute for the love that eludes them. The psychological benefits of love and holding values such as honesty, integrity, and loyalty have tremendous worth compared to things that can be purchased with dollars. Struggle and strength of purpose can give us happiness, even as the media encourages us to buy, buy, buy.

No pressure, no diamonds.
**~ Robert Griffin III, NFL Quarterback,
Kansas City Chiefs**

Enthusiasm and Growth

Show me a winner, a top sales person, or a great parent or student, and I will show you an enthusiastic person. Enthusiasm comes with focus. It requires the desire to succeed and the enjoyment that comes with it. A person with enthusiasm never asks, "What should I be doing now?" or "What do you want to do?" The following adjectives come to mind when I think of the enthusiastic people I have had the pleasure of knowing: passionate, happy, outgoing, and inspirational. These individuals are typically the leaders, never the followers. They always bounce back from adversity. Enthusiastic people ask what needs to be done and gladly do it. In relationships, they want to please the other person and put the interests of the other person first. At the office, they volunteer to do extra projects because they revel in the additional responsibility and challenge. Look around your office or examine your circle of friends. You know who the energy bandits are versus those who are enthusiastic. What are the common threads? Chances are the people who are always complaining and say it's never their fault—and that they are the victims of all outcomes—are the people with the least enthusiasm. They struggle in life while others seem to be on top.

Life isn't about finding yourself.
Life is about creating yourself.

~ George Bernard Shaw,
Irish Playwright

We are all born with enthusiasm. You have as much as anyone else. The real issue is how do you want to live your life? Are you willing to change and grow, or would you prefer to make excuses as to why others have it better than you or that they are happier because of _____(whatever)? If it's true that you are what you think about all the time, your results and quality of life will be directly correlated to the level of excitement with which you approach things. It's a mindshift. It's about changing your belief system as to who you really are. Many beliefs are typically lies about how weak and helpless we are in the face of life's opportunities and adversities. I say it's time to grab opportunity and create something wonderful rather than reacting negatively. How can you do this? Change your words, your language, and your thoughts, and remember to smile. You will begin seeing a whole new world, and it will be a world of opportunity and inspiration rather than a world of problems and challenges.

Your mind, heart, and soul need to be nourished daily. What have you been feeding yourself? Our thoughts create our feelings and beliefs; our feelings and beliefs lead to our actions; and our actions lead to results. So if you want to change your results, start by changing your thinking.

No one can make me feel inferior without my permission.

~ Eleanor Roosevelt, First Lady of the United States, 1933–1945

In his 2010 book, *You Can Choose To Be Happy: Rise Above Anxiety, Anger and Depression,* Dr. Tom G. Stevens states there are 3,600 seconds in an hour and 57,600 seconds in a normal 16-hour waking day. If we have one thought per second (which is much less than the brain's capacity), we have an approximate total of 60,000 thoughts per day. The average person has about 42,000 negative thoughts per day! How many do you have? Do you see the connection? Change your thinking and you change your life.

If you want to get depressed after a hard day's work, watch television. I avoid it. Sure I might watch the weather channel and some sports, but that's it. I avoid watching the news, because hearing about the political wrangling in Washington is depressing and disempowering.

I love listening to motivational tapes or reading success books by people such as Dale Carnegie, Tony Robbins, Zig Ziglar, Steve Chandler, and my other favorite, Norman Vincent Peale. Meeting successful people always inspires me, as does watching the Special Olympics or movies such as *The Blind Side, August Rush,* or *Slum Dog Millionaire.* Zig Ziglar states that 70 percent of all self-talk is negative and 70 percent of all illnesses are psychosomatic.

Reading books such as *The Four-Hour Work Week* by Tim Ferris, *Stress for Success* by James E. Loehr, and *Quiet Strength* by Tony Dungy is a better use of your free time than anything on television. These books will inspire you to get off the couch, set goals, and create a plan to reach them.

> **Enthusiasm is the mother of effort, and without it nothing good was ever achieved.**
> **~ Ralph Waldo Emerson**

The Company You Keep

Avoid socializing with negative people in or out of the office. These individuals are energy bandits who will suck the life out of you. Spend your time with positive, motivated, successful people. Eagles fly with eagles and skunks hang out with other skunks. Which do you want to be? One of my favorite tools when I hear petty gossip is to tell myself: *I don't care.* Try this simple technique so you can focus your mind on something more productive.

Too often, people use their lunch break as an opportunity to go out and commiserate with their co-workers. Your reward for this type of behavior is that you remain focused on everything you hate about your job. You also get to be bored with the food and from listening to the same old stories from your co-workers. Why would you do this to yourself? The people who do all the complaining also talk about how they don't even like each other—behind each other's backs, of course. Why are some people so masochistic? More to the point, why do people seem to go out of their way to make themselves feel horrible?

It takes just as much energy and time to feel good as it does to be miserable.

You can choose to use your lunch break as an opportunity for growth and development. For example, if you are in sales, go to lunch every day with a new prospect or a client. Take the top salesperson to lunch and learn how he or she has hit the big numbers and find out what they are currently doing to generate business. Be excited to learn, listen, and contribute.

Zig Ziglar states that you always have a choice. You can be happy or sad, optimistic or negative, hopeful or depressed. What do you choose? Whether you are consciously aware of it or not, you are choosing. The mind is like a rose garden. If you let the weeds get out of control, soon you will have all weeds. You are capable of mastering your own mind and applying this knowledge to your daily activities, your marriage, career, and health.

Change Your Routine, Change Your Results

When you head off toward a destination, you will need to make adjustments to stay on course, much like navigating a plane. Our moods go up and down with hormones, weather, seasons, work, and family events. By monitoring your feelings and thoughts, you can catch yourself before you go too far in the wrong direction and then adjust to get back on course. Early detection is the key. Once you get too deep into a downward spiral of negative thinking, it takes a lot of effort and time to reverse the trend. Know your body and mind, and remain aware.

Having coached hundreds of people, I've learned that monotony is perhaps the biggest factor that causes discontent and unhappiness. The routine of everyday life is often difficult and tedious. To break up the monotony, take a look at your daily life. Write down your routine during a normal workweek. What can you change? As author Kristen Moeller says in her bestselling book, *Waiting for Jack*, "How can you disrupt your ordinary?"

What aspects of living automatically can you change in order to stir things up and avoid boredom? Try taking a new route to work, eating your lunch outside, or inviting a co-worker you don't know well to share lunch with you.

Next, examine your weekends and vacations. This is your decompression time, during which you can rebuild your energy. Do you cherish these days and fill them with fun, physical activities that invigorate you, or are they filled with chores, "honey dos," and spacing out in front of the television? Most people exist rather than live! What about you? If I asked you to tell me about your past weekend, would I be bored or excited? Would I be eager to share your experience or would I yawn? Do you make plans or excuses? Stop blaming others, including your spouse, for your boredom and ask yourself: *What am I willing to change?*

Stop looking at others and thinking they have it better than you. The American Dream isn't about measuring yourself against everyone else; it's about creating the life *you* want—a life that reflects your values and authenticity. Find and stay true to your core. You need to worry about you and you alone. If you want to feel stimulated in your career and your relationship with your family, change your thinking and take action. Remember what I said about rewards and pleasures taking tremendous effort? It holds true here. To change your routine, and thus your results, you'll need discipline.

Discipline

Discipline, unfortunately, has become a dirty word to many people. To me, it's a beautiful thing, one of the many keys to a happy and productive life. Discipline is a regular practice we can exert in order to produce a specific result, character trait, or pattern of behavior. Discipline is a systematic method of obtaining obedience to something greater than our personality and immediate desires.

Sports legends such as Michael Jordan, Lance Armstrong, and Michael Phelps know that discipline is the difference between winning and losing. Jamie Dimon and Warren Buffet will tell you it's the key to building wealth. Martin Luther King Jr. exhibited tremendous courage and discipline in leading the movement for civil rights. In an interview on National Public Radio, comedian Jon Stewart credited discipline as the key to writing hilarious material for his hit comedy *The Daily Show*.

Most people apply very little discipline in their lives. If you don't believe me, let's look at a common problem in the U.S.—obesity. As of 2011, there were 12 states where the obesity rate is above 30% and in 38 states (76% of the states in America), the rate is over 25%. The latest studies by the World Health Organization ranked the U.S.A the fifth highest for male obesity at 31.1%. The latest findings by the American Council on Science and Health report (2011) suggests that today's children will be the first generation since the great depression projected to have a shorter life span than their parents. The American Council projects total health related costs to be approximately $344 billion by 2018!

Despite the facts and the health and economic impact to themselves, their families, and society, many people have little discipline when it comes to overeating, excessive alcohol consumption, drug use, and sexual behavior. Marriage has become a status of convenience more than a commitment. Quoting statistics is not as telling as taking a look at the people you know. How many are overweight and out of shape, smoke or drink too much, and/or have failed relationships?

The simplest things in life are often the most difficult. Call this a lack of judgment or lack of willpower, but it all boils down to lack of discipline. What can we do to instill more discipline in our lives? I have known professional athletes who are laser-focused on their training. Then again, I have known people who are disciplined about watching television, eating and drinking too much, and making laziness their profession. You are probably disciplined in some areas of your life, but which areas could be improved if you added a little discipline?

I'd like to conclude this discussion with an individual who has made the concept of discipline so simple. As a verb, "discipline" means to coach, educate, teach, or train. With these words in mind, let's learn about Sean Stephenson, an American therapist, self-help author, and motivational speaker.

Sean was born on May 5, 1979 with *osteogenesis imperfecta*, which is a genetic disorder commonly known as "brittle bone disease." He stands just three feet tall, but he is a giant among us all.

In a *Success Magazine* article dated December 2012, Sean talked about how he changed his life around and how his new bride got him to look for answers inside rather than turning to outside sources. The tools Sean uses to stay disciplined and create a happy, successful life are quite simple. He puts things into three categories: (1) Goals, Appreciations, and Preferences; (2) When Life Sucks; and (3) When Life Works.

The first category is self-explanatory. What are your goals? What do you want out of life? What do you appreciate? Make a list of the things you like doing that bring you the most joy, and then do them.

The second list, When Life Sucks, asks you to think about what you were doing when your life was miserable. What were you neglecting? Write these items on a piece of paper, but don't carry the list around with you because you don't want to be reminded of your misery. In fact, burn it.

Finally, focus on making Sean's third list, When Life Works. When have you been happy, successful, and healthy? What were you doing at the time? What were you eating? What activities were you avoiding? Post this list everywhere around you. Do whatever you need to do to remind yourself that if you want your life to work, you need to do what's on this list. Sean says that if you do everything on your list, you will be unstoppable.

Real Growth Requires Failure

The unknown can be scary, and with every new endeavor comes the natural fear of failure. People who have the ability to forge ahead past initial failures will achieve the highest degree of personal success. In fact, failure is a prerequisite for success. So why do so many fear it? What about failure scares you? Do you fear giving up your identity or self-image? Are you a perfectionist, and failure just isn't an option? Do you fear loss of status or respect if you try something and fail? Were you taught as a child that failure is unacceptable or shameful? Were you raised to avoid risk? Many corporate executives avoid any possibility of failure for fear they will lose future promotions or their jobs; however, the companies they work for often lose the competitive edge and suffer from their employees' lack of daring.

I have been through some terrible things
in my life, some of which actually happened.
~ Mark Twain, Author and Humorist

To recover your American Dream, you must be willing to fail, as everyone who has achieved any level of greatness will tell you. Adrian Savage wrote about it best in Lifehack Management (www.Lifehack.org) in 2007:

Trial and error is usually the prime means of solving life's problems. Yet many people are afraid to undertake the trial because they're too afraid of experiencing the error. They make the mistake of believing that all error is wrong and harmful, when most of it is both helpful and necessary. Error provides the feedback that points the way to success. No error means no success either.

Adopt New Thinking

The American Dream is about living a better life than your parents and leaving a better world for your children. My father never went to college. He was a lifelong employee of AT&T, and loyalty was everything to him. His philosophy was get a job, do your best, and stay there until you retire. My mom also valued loyalty. She married dad at age 16 and they stayed married for 59 years!

While loyalty is an admirable trait, my father's strategy of staying with one company through to retirement might no longer be viable in today's economy. Had I followed the advice that arose out of this type of thinking, I wouldn't have come close to the level of success I've experienced. Here are a few things my parents told me on the subject of how to be successful:

- Get a job in a good trade (like carpentry) and you will always have a job.

- Why would you leave U.S. Steel to become a stockbroker? You'll never make it selling stocks!

- Why would you leave Merrill Lynch when you are doing so well?

- If you leave Branch Management you will have to travel, and why would you want to do that?

Like all parents, they wanted what they thought was best for me. Most importantly, they hoped to protect me from failure. At some point, well-meaning family or friends may apply pressure to try to dissuade you away from your chosen path, and this influence may keep you from attaining your goals—if you allow it.

Before you begin any endeavor, you must vow not to give up at the first sign of failure. Think of Thomas Edison and Abe Lincoln, who both faced repeated failures before attaining their goals. Babe Ruth led Major League Baseball in both homeruns and strikeouts. The route to success is never straight up. In reality, it's more like a rollercoaster. So never give up! Never!

It's not how well you prevent potential mistakes or control events—because you can't— but how you deal with difficulties once they arise.

You can perceive your failures as evidence that you'll never succeed, or you can frame them in a positive light, take the lessons, and keep moving forward. If you want to recover your American Dream, I recommend the latter. My greatest victories were preceded by my greatest failures, which gave me the motivation and information I needed to move ahead in achieving my aims. When my family went on food stamps in 1968, for example, it led to my developing an incredible work ethic, a desire to make money, and the will to succeed. Adversity in high school led me to meet my mentor, H. Harry Henderson. Later, when the 1975 recession caused a glut in the housing market, it left me open to Mr. Henderson's suggestion that I give up the idea of becoming a carpenter and go to college. Growth through overcoming adversity is a pattern I have followed throughout my life.

Put Your Goals in Writing

The highly successful people I've met often have two things in common—they have a positive attitude and they write down their goals and measure the results. Decide what you will do or change in order to get results and write it down. Create goals that are realistic, yet pose a challenge. Have a plan, stay on task, and have a timeframe for completion. Work at a steady pace and be methodical.

First, identify or describe your goals in action terms. For example, if you want to get in shape, the action to take would be going to the gym three times a week. You must also remember that less is more and consistency is the key. Take small steps to achieve big results. You cannot get into great shape, lose 50 pounds, or go cold turkey with smoking or other bad habits in just a few days. The surest way to fail is expecting too much and going too fast. Thirty days makes something a habit, so consistency is crucial. Substitute good habits for bad in order to help your mind shift. What changes can you expect to see? What sort of shift might you feel when you are on the right track?

The key with any change is that it takes action and effort. Lying on the couch will not make you the next Ms. Olympia or the World's Strongest Man, but writing your goals on a piece of paper can get you started working on your goals.

CREATING YOUR CHART FOR CHANGE

1. Start by making a list of your long-term goals.

2. Next, list the actions you to plan to take in the first week to start working toward your goals.

3. List what you expect to accomplish in the first month.

4. List what you expect to accomplish in six months, in a year, and in five years.

Overcoming Procrastination and Feeling Overwhelmed

It's all well and good to say that you will get your finances in order, lose weight, stop smoking, or reach for any other worthwhile goal. The problem is getting started and then staying on track. The two biggest problems for most people are procrastination and feeling overwhelmed. How can we avoid these issues and accomplish our goals?

First, let's tackle procrastination. In this 24/7 world it's easy to be a worrier instead of a warrior. Rather than attacking the goal or problem, negativity sets in and we become frozen. We worry about our finances, the kids, health, and our relationships. We think rather than act. We go through the motions without any real productivity gains.

There is an easy way out of this dilemma. Whenever you feel yourself procrastinating or putting things off, ask yourself: *What should I be doing now?* Then take action. Movement, action, and decisive energy can solve almost anything. Action beats procrastination almost every time.

One word of caution when tackling procrastination: avoid being busy just for the sake of being busy. Ask yourself: *Am I being productive?* You might justify putting things off by telling yourself you didn't have the time. This is the "I'm too busy" excuse. You push papers, clean your office, return e-mails, and find other "stuff" to do. At the end of the day, you are exhausted with little to no gains in productivity. Work toward leaving the office with no (or very little) unfinished business.

Consequently, not only is it important to take action but the right activity is essential. Plow through the tough things first. Suffer if you must, but do what needs to be done. Look at your "to do" list. Are there things you have been putting off? All your unfinished business will weigh on you like a huge stone. Free yourself and you will feel the relief.

In conclusion, procrastination needs to be conquered by asking yourself the key question: *What should I be doing now?* Then do that one activity until it's fully completed.

With regards to feeling overwhelmed, realize that only thoughts repeated and believed can create these feelings. Do one thing at a time—the very thing in front of you at the moment—and in this way create simplicity. This puts *you* in control. Not in some distant future, but now. Stay in the present, slow down, and do the simple things great!

CHAPTER FIVE

The Five "Fs" to Balance: Fitness, Family, Finances, Friends, and Faith

Time is the most valuable thing a man can spend.
~ Theophrastus, Successor to Aristotle (372–288 B.C.)

Most of us never get caught up. Our in-baskets will never be empty. Cell phones, e-mails, the media, and other distractions keep us busy but not necessarily productive. Multitasking provides the illusion of productivity, but it prevents us from being present, and this leads to unnecessary mistakes. To gain control over your life requires you to control your time, which can only happen when you change the way you think and learn to prioritize. Time is never an issue if the task is important enough.

Make Your Time Count

When you prioritize your actions, the time you put in has a greater impact on results. Successful people do the things that others are not willing to do. Better to take on the toughest challenges first thing in the morning than to dread them all day. Disciplined people complete the difficult, intimidating, and untested tasks that move them closer to the life they envision *first*, before tending to the familiar, and usually louder, demands that keep people stuck in old patterns. At the end of each day, identify and write down three or four primary task items that you will complete the following day before you move on to the regular "stuff."

Do what's most important first.
~ Stephen Covey

Procrastination can destroy your dreams faster than any external obstacle. In the early 1980's, Merrill Lynch did a time and motion study, which concluded that the average advisor was on the phone about two hours per day. Financial advisors generate most of their revenue working the phones, so a reasonable question would be, "What are they doing with the other six to eight hours?" When I was supervising over 500 advisors more than 20 years later, my own analysis was about the same. Advisors make more money when they spend time talking to clients and prospects, so why don't they do more of it? Why do some choose to do nothing?

You set the priorities and you choose each day how you will live. Sometimes things happen that we can't control, but more often we pretend we are entirely affected by circumstances. We believe we are caught up in situations beyond our control. In fact, our thoughts, feelings, and actions set up situations for us to overcome. When we consciously choose priorities based on our values and allocate our time accordingly, a joyful and harmonious life unfolds.

You might say your life is too far out of balance to get it back, but this is not so. You can recover your dream of being happy, healthy, and prosperous. Even the slightest course corrections can create positive energy and help get you moving in the right direction.

A perfect example of why staying the course and giving that little bit extra is given by Sam Parker and Mac Anderson in their book *212: The Extra Degree*:

At 211 degrees, water is very hot; but raising the temperature just one degree makes water boil. The increase of one degree from 211 to 212 degrees makes all the difference in the world. It turns something that is very hot into something that generates enough force to power a steam locomotive. It's such a little increase, but it provides exponential results. The same holds true for your job and life. Let's imagine you are going to travel, but you are off one degree. If you walk just one foot and are off by only one degree, you will miss your target by .2 inches. This doesn't sound like much, but what if you are going further? After 100 yards, you would be off by 5.2 feet. After one mile, you would be off by 92.2 feet. If you were going to the moon, you would be off by over 4,000 miles! It's the little bit that can make such a big difference.

How many people are going through life not giving it that little extra? How many have the disease I call "the drift." This is what I see so many do. They start out with the best of intentions, but over time they keep giving their goals less attention and effort, and they end up with results that are far off the mark. They drift away from their original goals because they do not see immediate results, and they can't imagine how a little more focus and effort could make a difference. Take a look at how you service your clients or approach your relationships. Weight control is another perfect example. How many people can still fit into their college clothes? Likely, you have gained inches around your waist by eating a few extra calories with each meal.

How many people are in the gym in January vs. December?

So let's think about the number 212 and what just one degree of increase can make. Remember this message and take action. Be consistent and always make an extra effort in everything you do. This is how you will receive exponential rewards. The line between success and failure is so small that we are often on the line and don't even know it. The only thing that stands between a person and what they want in life is the will to try something and the faith to believe it's possible. Goals, time, energy, and commitment all go hand in hand. Begin today by thinking and acting differently.

Whether or not you do what it takes to have a better life, you are making a choice—and doing nothing is also a choice. If your entire day were going to be memorialized in tomorrow's newspaper, would you be proud?

The Five "Fs"

A balanced life doesn't necessarily mean your time is divided equally among these five areas, but the amount of time you devote to each should reflect your values. Let's figure out where you spend your time and how happy you are with the choices you make. Before you begin, let's look at an example.

If the imaginary person in the sample graph shown below is a wealthy "couch potato," he might rate his finances as a nine or 10, but fitness would get a zero or a one.

If he leads a faith-based life, the energy and time committed to this aspect of his life might be overwhelmingly greater than the others, and he would give it a 10.

If our imaginary person is fairly involved in activities and relationships at home, he might rate his experience with family as a seven.

Assuming his involvement with friends and his social circle rates a four, this is what the graph of our imaginary person would look like:

SAMPLE GRAPH FOR A BALANCED LIFE

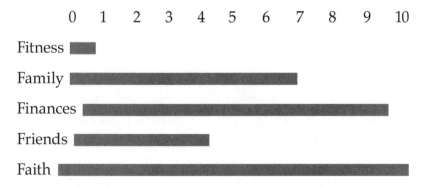

Now, it's your turn. Reflect on your level of satisfaction with each of these five areas and rate them 0 through 10. Fill in the graph below based on your feelings and experience. When you have selected a number for each of the five, shade in the area going across until you reach the number you selected. How craggy is the end of the bar graph? Is the allotment of your time balanced and in alignment with your values? Which areas need more focus and energy, and how might you cut back?

CREATE YOUR OWN GRAPH FOR A BALANCED LIFE

	0	1	2	3	4	5	6	7	8	9	10

Fitness

Family

Finances

Friends

Faith

Fitness

The physical and mental benefits of a hard workout are important elements that can help you recreate your life. One of my favorite sayings is "save the body to save the mind." Working out and keeping your body in good physical shape will give you the confidence and stamina you need to withstand the stresses of daily life and the workplace.

Exercise improves health, and without health you cannot provide for or enjoy your family, nor can you be productive in a career. Having fun is impossible when you suffer from health issues. A materialistic focus also impedes health, leaving your American Dream unfulfilled. Why? Because you spend all your time working or worrying about how you can afford or pay for the stuff you want or already have.

Corporate executives face arduous work schedules. For eight years, I traveled and held or attended meetings and conferences. Although I kept up an exercise routine to the best of my ability, I was tired. I spent the weekends trying to recharge my battery, give my family much needed attention, and catch up on paperwork. Good sleep came sporadically, and eating wisely was difficult.

The work hours for top echelon executives are even more time-consuming. Most of the people who run large corporations look old and tired relative to their age. If you are a doctor, lawyer, banker, or running your own business, you are probably on a work treadmill with no way to hit "pause." Even people who are realtors, salesmen, teachers, or secretaries are caught up in the rut of never having time for themselves.

How did we get into this mess? Wasn't a two-income household supposed to get you ahead in life? Didn't you believe your career would bring fulfillment and joy? Did any of us understand the unintended consequences of having too little personal time? Let's wake up and realize that striving to buy more stuff will not make us as content as creating some space in our lives to care for our loved ones and ourselves.

Whatever you do, give 110 percent but also organize and prioritize your time to allow for focusing on your health and exercising consistently. Do I miss some days? Of course, but my workout ritual is so ingrained that I am eager to get back to it. From the time I was 13, I've lifted weights and done push-ups and chin-ups. I was involved in sports growing up and enrolled in weight training in college. When I got my first job, I couldn't wait to buy a health club membership.

I always thought I was balanced and healthy—until my panic attack in 1994. It scared me, and I started looking for answers. Art Mortell coached me through the ordeal. He got me to go out and run on a regular basis in order to relieve stress. Running burns off cortisol, a stress hormone, and it stimulates production of serotonin and endorphins, which are the body's "feel good" hormones. It worked. I still use running or a good workout to burn off nervous energy.

Art also advised me to slow down in my other day-to-day activities. While "climbing the corporate ladder," I multitasked and did everything in a hurry. I always seemed to be running late and never seemed to have enough time. When I got home, I kept up the same pace until it was time to slow down and get a good night's sleep, which wasn't easy! Slowing the pace took conscious effort, and now I deliberately slow down while walking and talking, and I take time in between to reflect and rest. Slowing the pace has allowed me to focus better and avoid mistakes. Also, it has helped others feel more relaxed around me. Before I made this shift, my rushed attitude left other people feeling they were insignificant and that I had better things to do.

The brain can only focus on one thought at a time, so the best way to be efficient *and* have people feel heard and valued is to stay focused.

Actually, while the person in front of me was asking for help in solving a problem, I was thinking of everything all at once and trying to solve other problems. Be fully present with each individual and resolve the immediate issue to *completion* as quickly as possible. Then move on. It's the "incompletes" that drain our energy and distract us. Completion enlivens and energizes us. The secret is to go slow in order to accomplish more. How many incompletes are lurking in the back of your mind? Are you willing to slow down, get present, and complete them? Can you afford not to?

The practice of martial arts is a good way to find inner peace and relieve stress. Grand Master Sung Cho in Tae Kwon Do in Sarasota, Florida, near where I live, has taught me many lessons you cannot find in books. For about six years, I took private Tae Kwon Do lessons from him, striving to emulate this mighty warrior's extraordinary sense of inner peace. At the age of 58, he looked like he was about 25 years old. He lived a life of simplicity and balance. From my perspective, he appeared to live a life of ease, but that is also a testament to his skillfulness. Even though he taught hundreds of students each week, many of them children, he always appeared to be calm and centered. He had not contracted a cold in over 35 years. I often wondered how he managed to stay so healthy. The answer, he said, was quite simple: stay balanced in life, be mentally and physically strong, and eat right.

Master Sung Cho slept a solid eight hours each night, and if his schedule allowed it he took a nap during the day. He ate a banana in the morning and washed it down with plenty of water. Actually, he drank water all day. He ate fish with rice and vegetables at noon; a light snack around 3 p.m.;

and later a dinner similar to his lunch. He did not smoke or drink alcohol, and he advocated moderation in all things.

Doing anything too long or too much is unhealthy and creates stress.
~ **Grand Master Sung Cho, Tae Kwon Do Teacher**

At the time of my first lesson with Grand Master Cho, I thought I was in great physical shape. I was 35 years old, weighed 175 pounds, and could bench-press over 300 pounds. I played tennis and golf and jogged every other day. The reason for my visit was burnout. I felt terrible, could not sleep, and was generally unhappy.

Grand Master Cho tested my flexibility for the first 15 minutes. With no weights to lift and no sparring, I thought it would be easy, but after 30 minutes I could barely move. My legs were cramped and twitching. He looked at me and told me my body was very sick. "Americans work their whole lives, fill their wallets, retire sick, and die," he said. I started to think he might be right. I had money and success, but I could not touch my toes and was worried most of the time. Now, I was standing in front of someone more than 20 years my senior, who looked 10 years younger, and he was happy, calm, and could kick my butt. It made a big impression.

After my complimentary one-hour session, I sat in my car for about 10 minutes, waiting for my muscles to calm down so I could drive. All we had done were stretches and kicks, yet I felt as if I had just completed the Ironman Triathlon. I signed up for private lessons the next day. Over the course of my training, I got the most value from our conversations. I learned a great deal from Grand Master Cho about to how to live, and here are a few things that stuck with me:

- You are very flexible when you are born, but most people die with the inability to sit on the floor. Flexibility is the key that provides strength, health, and blood flow.

- Sparring is very good for the heart (non-contact).

- A brief nap every day is very healthy.

- Drink pure water all day and eat lots of fish and vegetables.

- Let your problems and the stress they create run off your back like water on a duck; otherwise, it will age and kill you.

- Stretch one-half hour per day. Grand Master Cho said he would probably not be able to do a split for the rest of his life if he stopped stretching for three consecutive months, because this is how fast the body atrophies and stiffens.

- Time spent weightlifting is more beneficial when combined with stretching.

- Balance is vital; too much of anything causes stress.

- Learn to control your thoughts and be calm.

- Smile all day.

Grand Master Cho helped me regain the two things I'd lost—balance and values. I realized there was more to the American Dream than just making a ton of money and working myself to death. I wanted to keep making money while it was possible, but I also knew I needed to have time for my family and other interests. The other important lesson was to prepare physically and mentally for stress and conflict. Life will always have its challenges, and we must learn to solve our problems in order to be successful. If you are strong in mind and body, you can deal with your difficulties more efficiently. I eventually earned a second-degree black belt, but I had to end my studies of Tae Kwon Do when I was promoted and began traveling for work.

While on a trip to New York City in 1995, I attended a lecture by Dr. Jim Loehr, who is one of the founders of what is now called the Human Performance Institute (HPI). Dr. Loehr spoke of the mind/body connection. He had coached numerous world-class athletes and helped them reach the pinnacle of their sport before he realized "corporate athletes" need to train harder and longer in order to endure a career that lasts 30 or 40 years, not just five or 10. Although professional athletes compete for a few minutes or perhaps a few hours each day, corporate athletes endure a grueling eight to 12 hours a day, every day, and in some cases even more.

Consider the indomitable relief pitcher Mariano Rivera of the New York Yankees. Mariano is a great person and a great ballplayer. He has a high-stakes, high-pressure job, but he only pitches every third or fourth day. Imagine if he had to perform at that level 40 to 60 hours a week! Dr. Loehr's speech resonated with my experience. I realized that pushing so hard was no longer a viable strategy. I wanted to become more efficient and nimble. I wanted to be healthy enough to enjoy financial independence once I attained it.

I visited HPI for a retreat at Lake Nona in Orlando, Florida, where I learned to create well-rounded workouts that included cardio, weights, and stretching, and adequate recovery time. I also learned proper nutrition strategies. For more information, you can read one of Dr. Loehr's 13 books, especially his bestseller *The Power of Full Engagement*. Here is some of what I learned from Dr. Loehr and the Human Performance Institute:

- Do at least 30 minutes of cardio exercise six days per week, and then rest for one day to let the body recover.

- Lift weights three to four times per week in order to maintain proper strength and bone density.

- Breakfast is the most important meal of the day; never skip it!

- Avoid caffeine unless you *must* have one cup of coffee in the morning. Again, everything in moderation.

- Cut out soda, candy, and all fast food.

- Be a grazer. Never let yourself get hungry, because it will help you avoid overeating. Try to eat every three hours, or so. It's better to eat badly than not at all. If possible, plan for the worst and always have healthy snacks handy, including fresh nuts, fruit, or meal replacement bars. The goal is to keep your glucose and energy levels stable.

- Stay hydrated; drink water throughout the day; and never go thirsty.

- Take one-minute mini-breaks every 90 minutes during the day; even a few seconds of rest is better than none at all.

- Be present with each activity; do one thing at a time.

- Make your daily workouts a habit, just as brushing your teeth or taking a shower and getting dressed in the morning are habits.

Maintaining health is fun and rewarding, so why isn't everyone physically fit? Why do people smoke, drink, or overeat, when everyone knows the health risks of these behaviors? Many successful people fail in reaching their goals because of poor choices and poor thinking. Regular vigorous workouts help balance your brain chemistry so you can feel great, think clearly, and make better choices. Take the Self-Quiz below to see how disciplined you are in supporting your health and well-being.

SELF-QUIZ TO TEST YOUR LEVEL OF DISCIPLINE

Ask yourself the questions listed below. Add up your "yes" answers and give each "yes" one point. If you scored 10 or more points, you are highly disciplined. Congratulations! If you scored eight or more points, you need a bit more motivation and discipline, but you are on the right track. A score lower than eight points means you have some major adjustments to make if you want to become fit. (YES = one point; NO = zero points.)

1. I eat small, frequent meals and never feel full or hungry during the day.

2. I drink at least six glasses of water per day.

3. I workout at least three times per week with weights.

4. I do at least 30 minutes of vigorous exercise daily.

5. I do not smoke.

6. I do not have more than one drink of alcohol per day.

7. I do not eat donuts, fast food, or other junk foods.

8. I get at least 7 hours of restful sleep each night.

9. I am within 10 pounds of my ideal body weight.

10. I am generally happy.

11. I live a balanced life.

12. I get an annual physical.

13. I eat a healthy breakfast every morning.

Most importantly, smile to lift your mood and make for a better day. Let the small stuff go. Smiling aides in relieving stress, lowers blood pressure, helps you stay positive, and releases endorphins, which will improve your mood. People want to associate and be with smiling people, not grumpy ones. A smile exudes confidence and increases effectiveness.

Thoughts affect behavior, and a bad attitude will only delay completion of a task and prolong the agony. Work diligently and be proactive to get through the tough assignments. Accept what comes along. Focus on the positive aspects of your job. Take a "get it done" stance rather than merely trying, and you will get the results you seek. Trying sets you up for stagnation and failure.

Do or not do, there is no try.
~ Yoda, Jedi Master in the *Star Wars* Trilogy

My father in-law, Bob Miner, always says, "If a problem or issue today will not exist in six months, let it go!" Richard Carlson's famed book *Don't Sweat the Small Stuff... and it's All Small Stuff* illustrates this point. Go back in time and re-examine the things you worried about in the past. Were they still significant challenges six months later? I'm willing to bet most (if not all) of them were resolved without effort.

I used to be proud of how little time I took off from work, to the degree that I made sure everyone knew it, my bosses as well as my peers. In my first 10 years of working, I took mostly long weekends off, no vacations. I never took two weeks off consecutively until I was nearly finished with my *career*. I learned the hard way back in 1995 that I *must* recharge my batteries periodically. From that point on, I took four weeks of vacation per year (one week every quarter). When you take time off and allow your emotional and physical resiliency to come to full charge, you can think clearly, calmly, and creatively. In the interim, take mini-breaks throughout the day. Before or after work, activities such as meditation, yoga, reading, napping, and taking a walk can bring about a sense of well-being.

Sleep

Our society is one of the most sleep-deprived in the world. The human body—especially the brain and nervous system—needs seven to eight hours of restful sleep in order to function properly. Reflect back on your own well-being during the times you were anxious, depressed, or ill, and your sleep patterns were disturbed. Waking up every few hours, or not being able to fall asleep or stay asleep, can lead to serious health issues. Often, exercise can help balance sleep patterns. However, if this does not resolve the issue, see a trained professional, because a serious health condition may be hampering your ability to get sufficient sleep.

Tips to help you get a good night's sleep, even under extreme pressure, include:

- Avoid all caffeinated products, especially after 6 p.m.

- Go to bed and get up at the same time each day, even on the weekends.

- Keep your bedroom temperature as cool as possible.

- Take 15 to 30 minute naps during the day when you need an energy boost.

- Never look at a clock when you wake up in the middle of the night.

- Keep your bedroom as dark as possible.

- Take a warm bath or Jacuzzi before you go to bed.

- Avoid stress, arguing, and dealing with issues prior to getting into bed.

- Beds are for sleeping and intimacy, not for working, arguing, or watching television.

- Your bed is not an animal shelter. Dogs and cats should have a separate area to sleep.

- Keep a pad of paper and pen at your bedside. If you have something on your mind, write it down with your eyes shut and then go back to sleep.

- Turn off your brain and let the neurons cool down. If you can't shut off your brain, think about happy things and places, or your favorite events.

- If you have to go to the bathroom, get up and go. Otherwise you'll just lie there uncomfortably thinking about it for 30 minutes and then get up and go anyway.

To attain the American Dream, we must strive to be successful emotionally and monetarily. Life is more fun wealthy than poor, and as one friend told me, "I'd rather be caught crying in a Mercedes than a "Smart Car." We need to provide for our families and allow future generations to enjoy a higher standard of living. But at what cost? Fitness and its corresponding health benefits are like a retirement account. You have to invest consistently every year in order to enjoy the benefits at a future date. Obesity, smoking, alcoholism, drug addictions, prescription drugs, and stress deplete this account. Your focus on fitness needs to receive the same intense attention as your quest for monetary success. It takes only 30 minutes a day, gives you energy, and allows you to enjoy all of the other aspects of your life.

Family

Loving relationships are the basis of personal happiness. We all want to love and be loved, and loneliness can shorten your life. Studies have shown that people in long-term relationships experience greater longevity and health. You can have wealth and health, but it would be for naught if you had no one to enjoy it with. I have been in a 25-year relationship with my wife, and our relationship and our two children are a big part of our American Dream.

In today's world of chauffeuring children, busy work schedules, and financial issues, it's no surprise that more marriages end in divorce than stay the course. After 21 years of marriage, I will be the first to say I'm no expert—I'm still trying to perfect the art of relationship. But, I will say that I have been blessed to experience many wonderful times with Nancy. She is patient and has put in the effort to keep us on-track.

A marriage is a relationship where you have two different people trying to live one life. Even though it's hard work, it's rewarding, because there is nothing better than sharing your life with another person.

Although marriage sometimes seems to get old, and the emotional and physical needs of both partners may not always be met, you have a lot invested so don't give up! Before you jump into divorce proceedings, why not work toward the goal of having a more fulfilling relationship with your current partner? Why substitute one set of problems for another?

If you are unhappy in your marriage, make reading the following guide books mandatory: *Relationship Rescue* by Dr. Phillip C. McGraw, Ph.D. and *Getting the Love You Want* by Harville Hendrix, Ph.D. The exercises in these two books will require an investment from you and your partner, but anything worthwhile takes time and commitment.

To improve your marriage immediately, ask yourself two questions each morning when you wake up: *What can I do to please my partner? What can I do to keep my partner in my life?* When was the last time you asked yourself this type of question? When was the last time you had a date night with your spouse? Do you want to be one of those couples that go out to dinner and eat without saying a word? Do you want a meaningful relationship that fulfills your emotional and physical needs, or do you just want to coexist?

Start by getting out of the routine. Turn off the television and look into your spouse's eyes when you talk to one another. Learn to laugh and find out what is going on in your partner's life. Workout and spend time outdoors together, and create intimacy as often as possible. You married each other for a good reason—relearn why! In addition to setting goals for fitness, your career, and perhaps your finances, also include your marriage. Begin by sitting down with your spouse and creating a Relationship Vision as described in *Getting the Love You Want*. When Nancy and I did this exercise, it reminded me of the movie *The Bucket List*. After creating our vision, we reminded each other every week of the reasons we wanted to be together.

When we read our list aloud, it makes us feel good and draws us closer. Everyone needs to feel loved and appreciated. It's not complicated. Take a little time and make an effort to discover how your partner wants to be treated, and then invest your time and effort accordingly.

If Nancy and I have made mistakes, it would be the times we let the children or our careers supersede our marriage as a priority. We have since realized that our relationship is the hub of our life, and all our other priorities are the spokes. It's easy to get caught up in the competitive nature of the workplace or the kids' hectic schedules, but keeping your priorities straight will ensure a happier marriage and family. Children want the security of a solid relationship between their parents, and everyone wants the security of a solid loving relationship.

When it comes to family, children play a tremendous role. There has been nothing more gratifying than family vacations, holiday celebrations, and the activities we share— from sporting events at school to the hunting, diving, and biking we do as a family. These activities bond us. Our time spent together also helps keep communication open as the kids get older and begin to seek independence. By staying active, you can keep the excitement in your family as well. We have made our home the central place for our children's friends to hang out, which keeps us engaged and aware of what they are doing and with whom.

Over the years of raising our children and watching my

friends raise theirs, I've witnessed or experienced two main areas of concern: spending too little time with the kids or being overly involved and spoiling them. The first mistake Nancy and I made was spoiling them. Growing up with very little made me want to give my children everything and solve all their problems for them. Yet, they needed to develop their own problem-solving skills in order to become productive adults. So give your children responsibility before you give them their freedom.

Nancy and I came from different social backgrounds, and we have not always acted as a team in parenting. The kids sensed this and used the strategy of divide and conquer to get their way. This wasn't so much of a challenge when they were young, but issues such as curfews, driving, friends, and activities were difficult to navigate when they got older and Nancy and I were coming at it in different ways. We developed a "good guy, bad guy" relationship with the kids versus holding a united front. This put a strain on our relationship and actually hurt the children, who needed to be given consistent messages and learn healthy boundaries. We discovered that our relationship must be the center of the family and that we must be aligned with each other in parenting and making decisions. Once we accomplished this, we were able to teach our children they are not entitled to *everything*. The world does not revolve around them. They must be held accountable for their own decisions. They need to work hard for things they want and learn to solve their own problems.

Now, we run the family in a business-like fashion. We have rules and stick to them. The kids might not like certain decisions, but they respect them. There's no definitive manual on parenting. It's trial and error, and we do our best to make decisions out of love. Teenagers can put a strain on your marriage if you let them. Tough love and consistency helps them feel like home is a safe place and they can always talk to us about anything. Many times you get it right, but sometimes you get it wrong. The key is to stay united with your spouse and firm in your family values and rules. You and your spouse might not always agree on how to parent. You eventually learn that you are not right or wrong, and neither is your spouse. It's fine to seek advice from friends, but realize that you will likely tell them only what validates your views (not your spouse's), and that this can lead to confusion and angst between partners. Parents need to be united as one unit and act as the children's best coach—not their best friend!

There are numerous books and school-sponsored speakers on child rearing, but we have found *The Total Transformation Program* by James Lehman to be the most valuable. Although it's billed as a parent's program for managing challenging behaviors, we have found it to be much more. We learned how some of the things we did out of love confused our children, such as not setting rules, negotiating behavior, fully rewarding incomplete work, downplaying responsibilities, weak consequences or overly harsh ones, only focusing on our agenda vs. theirs, and much more. This program takes two months to work through, but it's worth it.

I had another friend who worked tirelessly climbing the corporate ladder. He announced with pride that he took his kids on a vacation of their choice once a year. What about the other 51 weeks? Whose American Dream is *that*? Is that what you really want? To have your kid feel such a void because you work all the time that he or she would give anything for a few hours with you? I doubt it.

When you place your career over everything else, your children suffer. I had one friend who asked his 10-year-old son what he wanted for his birthday, and his son's reply was, "I just want my dad!"

Both of these men are fabulously wealthy, but they did not experience their children growing up. The kids are now in college and the childhood years are gone. They have more money in the bank than I do, but I feel richer for the time I've spent with my family.

You cannot buy love and time, and kids grow up fast. There are only a small number of years when they'll ask for your attention. After that, if they didn't get it, they're gone—and you'll spend your later years wondering why they never call. It's a matter of choice. What is most important to you? This is where you get to check your ego at the door and decide. Johnny Walker, a famed fishing captain in Sarasota, Florida advises, "Take your kids fishing so someday they will take you." This says it all.

In sum, a solid marriage and family is the foundation of the American Dream. Experiencing the Five "Fs" with the people you love the most is infinitely rewarding. There will be challenges to overcome and choices to make. At times, it will require patience and effort, but putting family first creates greater joy and prosperity, and your children will grow into healthy, successful adults.

Finances

The American Dream was built on the concept of *Life, Liberty, and the Pursuit of Happiness.* Unfortunately it has become Life, Liberty, and the Pursuit of *Stuff.* Jefferson and Franklin could never have imagined the out-of-control materialism reflected in modern society. The quest for possessions has grown beyond extremes, so far that even life and liberty now take a backseat. Many people would rather die or be shackled with lifelong payments to creditors than give up (or even wait to purchase) material goods.

Although it's true that to buy something you can't afford is almost never a good idea, it's worth mentioning that just because you can afford to buy something doesn't mean you should. I know people who buy purses for $2,000. I know of one woman who sent her dry cleaning from Florida to New York! I have other friends who don't even worry about whether they can afford something. They are constantly leveraging themselves higher with houses, boats, and cars, and they keep little in savings. Their desire to look good has overcome their common sense, and even their sense of self-preservation. Some have racked up credit card debt in excess of $100,000! These individuals are attorneys, doctors, and business owners. They are smart, hardworking, and highly educated. Now in their 50s, they feel so broke they often say, "I'll never be able to retire, so I might as well live for today." This is not living; this is not enjoyment; and it certainly isn't the American Dream! It's a life sentence of pressure and anxiety.

Being in the unique position of reviewing or monitoring the financial statements of highly successful people—

and having spoken with hundreds of families about their finances, feelings, and investment risk tolerance—I've come to the following conclusions. The wealthiest and happiest people:

- Live well below their means and have little or no debt.
  Whatever the dollar amount, people with savings are in the best mood.

- Create and stick to a budget.
  Track your monthly income and plan your expenses. Having more going out than coming in is not good. If possible, have at least six months of living expenses readily available and save at least 10 percent of your income with a goal of 20 percent. In other words, for every dollar you earn, you need to save 10 cents. The key is to differentiate between what you truly need and what you desire.

- Invest wisely.
  Make sure most of your investments are safe and you're earning a fair return. Invest with knowledgeable professionals.

- Provide for retirement and have insurance.
  Protect your family in case of an untimely accident or death.

- Always maintain a degree of liquidity.
  If you need to sell, when can you get your money? Many a painful lesson has been learned in real estate, limited partnerships, or closely held businesses. Arrange your investments in such a way that you can make a call

and sell immediately, and know in advance the price and amount you will receive from the sale. Long-term investments—and even lifelong investments—are fine as long as you can comfortably afford them.

- Control their money.
  Never invest with an individual who controls your funds. Don't allow greed to cloud your judgment. I have seen countless investors lose $500,000, or more, trying to make $100,000. Sound investments take time and patience.

- Know their risk tolerance.
  I have always been conservative by nature, which has served me well. It did not take too many bad stock deals for me to realize I work too hard for my money to blow it on a gamble.

- Have a plan.
  You may work 50 to 60 hours a week and spend only a few hours of the year planning. If you spend 2,000 to 3,000 hours per year earning your money, it makes sense to spend at least 10 hours planning for a rainy day and future enjoyment. A few hours of planning can help you avoid days or months of needless worry. Charitable considerations and legacy planning should also be part of your long-term financial plans.

Take a look at your personal situation. At this point in your life, you are likely successful in a career, which is the key vehicle for getting you to financial independence. It doesn't matter if you are a carpenter, plumber, physician, or an entrepreneur. You believe you are competent and professional, and you rate yourself highly in your skill. However, you might also be frustrated, bored, overworked, or a combination of all three. Although your paycheck may be less gratifying, your ability to save, invest, and build wealth begins with having some money to start. If possible, take 20 percent of your money and sock it away. If not 20 percent, take 10 percent or even five percent, but save something. Commit to developing the habits of the wealthiest, happiest people, and the financial piece of your American Dream will be within reach.

Fun

One area that I've consistently underrated in my life is having fun. The rigors of working to elevate my social class have demanded a lot of long hours. With today's hectic pace, it's tough to find the free time to have some laughs. After leaving work and rushing to activities for the children and then finishing the household chores, by the time we can kick back Nancy and I are often physically and mentally exhausted.

Relaxing and enjoying the moment might seem like yet another "to do" on your list, but it's a necessity. Having fun allows the neurons in your brain to cool down. Spending time with friends is a vital part of having fun. Make a list of the activities that bring laughter into your life, and try to incorporate at least one of them into your daily schedule.

Until recently, lengthy family vacations were not a part of my schedule. Even long weekends don't allow enough time to unwind. I did not take my first two-week vacation until I was 46, and I'm not proud of it. If you can afford to spend the money, you can afford the time. You need at least one solid week off per quarter—preferably somewhere your Blackberry®, cell phone, and other electronic gadgets don't work.

The perfect family vacation includes plenty of exercise. Skiing, fishing, diving, mountain biking, and hiking are great ways to have fun and reconnect with your family. Create traditions and cherished memories by picking favorite activities you can do together. Fun does not have to be complicated; it can be anything that gives you enjoyment, helps you relax, and allows your mind to unplug. Fun is not about thinking—it's about being in the moment and enjoying life. It's different for every person. Whatever you perceive as fun is not as important as making sure you have enough of it. Here are some helpful guidelines:

- Laugh often, laugh loud, and laugh often.

- Create rituals that help you relax and keep you feeling centered.

- Perform random acts of kindness to enrich your life and that of others.

- Be optimistic and focus on the positive.

- Be present in each moment. Fun time is for fun and only fun. There's always time to fret when you go back to work or other performance-driven activities.

Whatever you're doing, if it isn't fun you're not doing it right.

~ Fran Tarkenton, The Great NFL Quarterback

Friends

Modern society does not lend itself to building close, strong friendships, and many people say they can count their good friends on one hand. Unfortunately, this has been true in my life and for so many others I've known.

When the firm I was working for treated the Executive Team to a three-day retreat at Dr. Loehr's Human Performance Institute, approximately 30 Senior Managers attended. These people were responsible for running the brokerage side of the business. Their hours were long, the demands on them high, and time was a scarce commodity. The average income of the participants was in excess of one million dollars a year.

There was one exercise that focused on doing a "reality check" to determine what was really going on in our lives. Some of the most powerful people on Wall Street sat in the room. Many Americans would have been envious of the attendees and assumed they were happy, well-adjusted, and high-functioning individuals. For the most part, they were.

We took turns talking about our individual visions about how we wanted to interact with our friends and family. We talked about what was going on for us and how we wanted our lives to unfold. The discussion became very emotional. Some voices quivered and others cracked as tears rolled down their cheeks. Why? With few exceptions, these Wall Street tycoons realized they had few, if any, friends, and that they had neglected their families.

Everyone in the room seemed to realize that business success had cost our personal lives dearly. We knew something had to change. We longed for more fun, more friendships out of the office, and closer relationships with family members. It's so easy to get on the hamster wheel and keep running. Tomorrows accelerate into years, as we strive to climb the corporate and social ladder. We lose our grounding in reality—what is most important fades from our awareness. As we gain more prestige, responsibility, and net worth, we lose part of the American Dream. At some point, the cost/benefit ratio gets skewed to the negative, and we might not even know it unless we have the courage to look. Is it time for your reality check? What have you been neglecting?

Everyone in the group made a commitment to get back in touch with lost friends, rekindle the spark with their spouses, and spend more time with their kids. I know I did! I felt as if my soul had been cleansed and I was going to be different. Yet, after a few hours at work the following Monday, the best of my intentions were lost as I stared at the in-box that never seemed to be empty, the mass of conference calls, and numerous other problems.

How often has something like this happened in your busy life? Whether you're working on your health, creating more family time, trying to squeeze in a date night, or just hoping to take some time off, things never seem to happen as planned. The point is that as significant as friendships are, they often take a low priority. As much as we love our parents, siblings, spouse, and children, there's no substitute for a trusted friend. Friends can hear the information we would be embarrassed by or feel unable to discuss with family members. Issues with sex, marriage, kids, and work-related problems at times are better first discussed with friends. A good friend can offer help and objective advice when problems arise. Many activities are more fun with a friend.

When we are stressed, we just need someone to listen, not give solutions or add controversy. Friends fill this void.

True friends accept your faults, are happy for your successes, and sad for your misfortunes. Good friends never lie or have ulterior motives. They enjoy your company and you enjoy theirs. Friendships take little work because there is a shared interest and desire for being together. After your immediate family, friends care about you the most.

Good friends are like your old room in your parents' house. You might not see or feel its comforts for a while, but when you go home you feel like you never left. I am blessed to have five lifelong friends like this. I might not see or talk to them for months, but when we get together it's like we've never been apart. We've been through good times and bad, happiness and tragedies, and we can always count on each other. Friends make an effort to stay connected and are not mad if you are busy and don't always make the effort. There are little to no expectations. They expect nothing in return except your friendship. Friends make you feel good, important, and respected, and they bring about a rise in your self-esteem. Friends ground you and help you realize what's truly important. A good friend will never take advantage of your friendship, because the cost of losing it would be far too great. They trust you and you trust them. This mutual respect is priceless and rare.

People sometimes pretend to be friendly just to take advantage. I know people who only associate with those who can provide business or referrals. They try to get into your network to take advantage of your friendships with others for their own monetary or personal benefit. Once I no longer had my position as an executive, I found out quickly who my true friends were. Many people stopped calling and some would not even return my phone calls right away. Once they realized there was no advantage, they distanced themselves and became too "busy." These are not friends.

A large study published in the *British Medical Journal* was conducted to monitor survival rates over a 10-year period. It compared family ties versus strong personal networks or friendships. The conclusion was that close ties with children and other family members appeared to have no impact on longevity. However, survival rates were much higher for the participants with a strong network of close friends and confidants than for those with weaker friendships. One conclusion was that family ties are often maintained out of a sense of obligation, but friendships are a matter of choice and thus more invigorating.

Finding true friends is not easy. If you are a highly successful person, you are likely to associate with people of a similar socioeconomic background. If they are not co-workers, perhaps you met them through your children's school, your neighborhood, or your place of worship. While it takes little effort to maintain strong friendships, it takes real effort to develop new ones. Had I had the foresight, I would have started developing more friendships prior to leaving the workforce. When I retired from my job, I couldn't hit golf balls anymore, and the majority of guys my age were still working. Build up a network of friends prior to middle age, or you may find the second half of your life disappointing and lonely.

If you are a married man and have a difficult time finding friends, you can meet people through your spouse, because women are often better at socializing than men, or you can join an activity club, organization, or country club. Charitable organizations and spiritual communities offer social opportunities as well as the deep satisfaction of supporting something you believe in. The key is to get involved.

Although I am as busy as ever, I don't waste time with individuals who are looking only for economic benefit and don't share my values. Your time is limited, so don't be fooled by those who only want to benefit and give nothing in return. Make an effort to develop a network of friends, people with similar interests, backgrounds, and values. Friends will improve your relationship with your partner and your health, and you'll have more fun.

Finally, I have discovered that a pet can be an invaluable friend. My dog Lucky was a big black Lab and my true friend for 11 years. She had so many characteristics of what a friend should be. She was loyal, trustworthy, friendly, happy, and always at my side—especially if food was involved! Pets have been known to provide healing benefits, security, companionship, and happiness. Lucky taught me that I should never take anything for granted, especially a good friend.

My American Dream is a journey to be shared with friends. Everything is more enjoyable with people you trust, respect, and love. Time spent developing friendships will pay huge dividends as you strive to create your American Dream.

Faith

Faith is the number one value in my life. It's my moral compass and strength. I was raised Catholic, and as an altar and choirboy I attended mass six days a week while growing up. As an adult, I attend mass two to three times a year, yet my faith is stronger than ever and I pray daily.

I am not a religious zealot, but I do believe in a creator, heaven, and life hereafter. I rarely speak about religion with others, because religious and political conversations seem to be the quickest way to lose friends.

Regardless of which path you choose, we are all blessed to practice our religious faith in the United States without fear of persecution. The American Dream includes liberty and the freedom to speak and believe our own truth.

In God We Trust

The first major test of my faith occurred when I was a sophomore in high school. I was taught to go to confession and tell the priest about my sins and bad thoughts, and then receive penance. I made the trip to the confessional monthly throughout grammar school, but only quarterly once I reached high school. The priest gave penance, which usually included instructions to complete a handful of prayers, ask for God's forgiveness, and say you will never do it again.

On one of my trips to the confessional, I told the priest I had missed mass. He really let me have it, telling me that I was not worthy to be a Catholic. I felt terrible and thought I would go to hell or purgatory, at best. I left the confessional and knelt for about half an hour praying and asking forgiveness.

The next week, I still felt guilty. I knew same priest was giving mass, because I always tried to figure out the voice and person behind the confessional screen. After mass, my dad drove us to the local store to get groceries, where we witnessed the same priest jump out of his car, get into a convertible with a young lady, and begin to kiss her! Long story short, the next week the priest ran off with another man's wife.

Talk about a test of faith! The man who had been so hard on me for missing one week of mass was committing adultery! I learned from this experience that faith is not to be placed with another person or in a church. Faith is the basis of the direct relationship between the individual and God. It exists in the human heart and soul.

After high school and into my early adult years, my faith ebbed and flowed according to my circumstances—I prayed hard when I needed something, and I didn't pray when things were fine. About 20 years ago, that changed.

In September of 1990, I got a call from my mother that my brother was in intensive care in an Orlando Hospital. She said he'd had a severe stroke and the doctors weren't sure if he would survive, and if he did survive no one was sure how well his brain was going to function. He was a great athlete in his early 30s with two small children and a young wife, and it seemed inconceivably unfair. My brother was also exceptionally smart and had been a rocket scientist for Martin Marietta. His brain injury meant the end of his career—in the same way a spinal cord injury would end the career of a professional athlete.

I waited at the hospital for a couple of days. We were asked to decide whether to pull life support and bring in a priest to administer Last Rights. It was traumatic for all of us. I spent a lot of time in the hospital chapel praying, as there wasn't much else I could do to help. I asked God lots of questions in that chapel. "Why did you let this tragedy happen? If you truly are all powerful, why won't you make him better?" Then I prayed that the Lord would take him, because I didn't want him to suffer in a permanent vegetative state. Even when I had no clue as to what might happen, I did not give up on God. I prayed for strength and asked God to help my parents get through it. I asked God to help my brother's wife and children. What was His plan? What purpose did my brother's stroke serve?

My brother somehow made it out of that hospital bed alive. He still has no use of one arm, walks with a slight limp, and has broken speech. When he woke up, he kept asking over and over, "Why, why?" Medically, he had a hole in his heart that filled with clotted blood, broke free, and lodged in his brain, causing the stroke. But, the real answer to his question cannot be known, because only God knows what is in store for us.

I lost part of my brother when he had his stroke, but I thank God he is still alive and has been able to see his two girls grow up and graduate from college. He is determined to go back to work as a rocket scientist someday. I don't know if that will ever happen, but I do know his hope keeps driving him to do what most of us complain about: go to work! He works tirelessly to speak more clearly, to walk better, and regain use of his arm. My brother is a real inspiration. I feel sad that we cannot play golf or basketball, or do any of the other things we did together as kids, but I'm thankful that I can still see him and speak with him.

Rather than shaking my faith, this event strengthened it. As devastating as my brother's illness was, and continues to be, I have faith that he and his family are being watched over by God. No one gets through a lifetime without experiencing the sorrow of illness and death, but we all have so much to be thankful for as well. I no longer have a one-way relationship with God. He is not there just for tragedies and to hear complaints. I believe in prayer as my source to stay connected to God.

My core begins and ends with my faith and belief that each of us has a divine destiny. Helping my immediate family and the other people who cross my path fulfills my destiny. I trust in God's plan. That which many call luck or chance is nothing more than God bringing grace and us together.

Be Happy with What You Have

The road to success runs right through a town called "Failure," because no one gets to the top without a lot of hard work and disappointments along the way. Faith gives us the strength and the ability to get through hardship and come out stronger, wiser, and with greater compassion. We must *expect* good things to happen. Out of big problems come bigger opportunities. How many times have things looked bleak only to turn out better than you expected?

We are living in hard times, with foreclosures hitting record levels. America's manufacturing base is in decline and deficits are soaring. Consequently, you may be having financial or marital difficulties and struggling with family, health, and career issues. I truly hope this is not the case and you are happy, healthy, and prosperous.

Being happy with what you have acknowledges that what you have is all you need.

I have received many blessings, but I have also had my share of unanswered prayers. Sometimes, I learned later that *not* getting what I thought I wanted was the blessing. I believe this goes to the core of my message: be happy with what you have. When you acknowledge that you have everything you need, you get to feel abundant. Whether you have $5 in your pocket or $50 million in the bank, quit worrying about what you don't have. If God wants you to have something, you will be granted your desire if you have faith and pray for it— and you're willing to give something of value in exchange. If you receive what you desire, be happy. If you do not receive it, be happy. Sure, you can keep asking, but don't brood over not getting it. Be thankful and move on. Perhaps God's plan for you is different, something even better. The key is not to live a depressed, unhappy life because you are so focused on what you don't have.

God wants every human being to live a rich and fulfilling life. It's okay to ask for money, prestige, and material goods—this is not selfish. We are all created in God's image, and we all have divine potential. Dare to dream bigger. Ask for big things in your life and have the faith that you will receive. If you fall short, I guarantee you will be farther ahead than if your goal was minuscule.

I have always dreamed big, but perhaps I should have dreamed even bigger. God has given me so much of what I have asked for, but I continue to ask for more because I know there is always more to receive. So have faith that God will provide the gifts you desire and show you the way to accomplish your goal.

The key to faith is that it cannot be a one-time event. Most people become very religious when they are in trouble or want something. Faith must be a daily practice. It grounds and guides us, and brings us joy and heals our sorrow. We each have a responsibility to stick with whatever faith guides us to. Faith and prayer can bring about change. Words of gratitude and asking for God's continued blessings will indeed reap rewards. Think victory and success, and you shall receive. The key is that you have to ask. When was the last time you asked God for a blessing? When was the last time you asked God to bring your dreams to pass?

Hope is a healing medicine that needs no prescription. Faith allows you to stay hopeful, positive, and strong. Faith gives you the positive mental attitude to see things through and work out your difficulties, so build your life on faith.

As you determine how you will recover your American Dream, I urge you, as Covey said, to "begin with the end in mind." You came into this world naked and with nothing, and you will leave the same way. Wrap yourself in your faith. It's the only thing you get to keep.

Putting the Five Fs to Work for You

As of this writing, America is experiencing one of the biggest financial crises since the Great Depression. Never have we had so much but felt so poor. To recover your American Dream, you must take personal responsibility for your own finances. Learn to live below your means and avoid the scourge of debt. If you are enslaved by too much debt and too many possessions, the American Dream will forever elude you. Your attention will be wasted on items that matter very little in the end. If we wait for Washington to solve things, we will be waiting a long time. It's our collective problem, not the problem of the politicians.

If you believe you can only find happiness in material possessions, your American Dream will be unattainable and you will never be content. Fitness, family, finances, friends, fun, and faith cost nothing. Commit to this mind-set and focus on these values. They are attainable by all people, regardless of race, religion, income, or social class. The American Dream is at hand for all of us.

CHAPTER SIX

What Are You Waiting For? Start Now!

Life isn't about finding yourself. Life is about creating yourself.

~ George Bernard Shaw, Irish playwright and co-Founder of the London School of Economics

Robin Hoffman, my writing coach, used to tell me, "Just get going. You can always make changes later." Once you are in motion, inertia will help carry you forward. To begin takes courage, which then requires discipline to stay the course. But if you wait, your goals may never manifest.

Many of you reading this book already know how to keep going until you reach your goals, or you wouldn't have obtained success in your current profession. What I am asking from you now is renewed discipline in order to make your career and other valuable areas of your life more rewarding and enjoyable.

Focus on creating rather than reacting. Set your own attitude toward appreciating what you have, and believe you can have what you want. Change requires discipline and persistence. It requires a change of thinking. Understand the power of your mind and learn to control your thoughts. To succeed, you cannot give up when the going gets tough.

Remember, failure precedes success, and you cannot demand immediate gratification. Certain changes require a lot of time and effort. If you need to lose weight and get in shape, it will take months, not minutes. So just get started. Embrace the thought that today you will begin a new life.

The joy is in the journey. Always be hopeful and optimistic, but also expect setbacks along the way. The benefit of measuring your progress is that you can track your results from the beginning to a certain point in time. To recreate yourself and recover your American Dream is to permanently alter what you do and how you think. If it were easy, everyone would already be doing it. You cannot change the past or put the "broken egg" back together, but you can act in the moment and do your best to influence the future. You can only lose or fail if you don't start or you quit. The only questions are: *What are you willing to do? What do you really want?*

Each person will likely make at least five key decisions over a lifetime: career, life partner, whether or not to have children, health, and finances. If you can make these decisions wisely and with a clear frame of mind, you are certain to experience greater happiness. To fully recreate your life takes courage, time, and effort.

**The temptation to quit will be greatest just
before you are about to succeed.**

**~ Chinese aphorism quoted by Bob Parsons,
CEO and Founder of GoDaddy.com**

Give up feeling overwhelmed, and have faith that the roadblocks *will* go away. Begin your new life today. Move the ball forward, believing in yourself and the endeavors you wish to undertake. Don't expect a magic genie to appear or some outside event to trigger instant change. It's up to you to do your part to recover your American Dream.

Which area in your life would you like to improve? Pick one. Just one! Next, train your brain. Focus on the specific area as if it were something you have already accomplished many times. Michael Jordan did not achieve success by avoiding the basketball court. Move forward confidently and methodically, and repeatedly execute the *process* of accomplishing the task. Repetition breeds success.

The key is not to focus only on the problem in front of you. If you do, pebbles become boulders. You will become frozen. Just start the process. At night, my mind often takes off in its own direction, examining incomplete tasks and searching for solutions. Creative ideas emerge that fuel my enthusiasm and motivate me to resume my efforts the next day. Focus on an activity you believe will get you one step closer to where you want to be. Be present with it, complete it, and move on to the next action.

Mind-Set

Each of us can alter our lives by changing our mental attitude. Changing your focus and priorities will alter outcomes. Forget the past. Focus on where you want to go right now and where you want to end up. Ask yourself: *What do I really want?*

Managing your own thoughts will begin to change how you feel. You cannot overestimate the power of a positive mental attitude. Think happy to be happy. It's that easy, but oh so difficult. Old habits must die, and it takes vigilance to let go of them. You have to consciously focus on improving your thinking every waking moment. You cannot afford one negative thought.

Your mind is a complicated, self-tuning machine that prefers the status quo. Just like your brain controls your bodily functions in an effort to keep the organism stable, the mind prefers to engage the same thought patterns over and over throughout the decades. The important thing to know is that your higher consciousness can direct your thoughts away from old patterns and create new ones. You are in control. With practice, you can change the way you think, how you react, the way you perceive others, the way you view the world, and how you experience your life. When you change your perception, you change your thoughts, which shifts your feelings. This, in turn, alters your actions and transforms your life. It took years for you to get to where you are now. Change won't happen overnight, but it won't take as long to make progress as it took you to get where you are. I can promise you that!

Letting Go

Recovering your American Dream requires you to let go of the past and take action in the now—and remember the best part about the past is your ability to forget it.

Start by forgetting how much your portfolio has shrunk, what you used to have in the stock market and your

401(k), or whatever your house was worth at the height of the last bubble. Lose the mind-set that it's too late, that you blew it, that you will never have financial independence or lose weight or have close relationships, or whatever it is that you think is missing. Just let it all go. Acknowledge what happened, forgive yourself, and move on.

We all have baggage. If you are bogged down with negativity and anxiety, deal with the underlying thoughts. Do what must be done to let them go. Work on your mind-set and get help if you need it. One way or another, to recover your American Dream you've got to let go of the past. When I coach individuals, health and finances are the two dominant themes. These issues arise regardless of income. The financial piece is completely within your control. Chances are, no one reading this book will go hungry or without shelter; at least I hope not. So what's the problem? What keeps you up at night? Perspective is a wonderful teacher.

If you lost your job or your home during the economic downturn, you have been given an opportunity to change course. What have you always dreamed of doing? What can you do to bring it to fruition? Can you do it part-time? The greatest inventions and breakthroughs come out of hard times. You owe it to yourself, your family, and society as a whole to explore what's inside of you.

What is your big idea?
Where can you create opportunity?

Relationships are critical to your emotional state. A healthy relationship with your spouse or significant other will provide support. The key is that you need to make sure the relationship is secure, enjoyable, and loving. You cannot expect the other person to provide for your needs above all else. Make sure you have a network of friends, so your spouse doesn't have to shoulder the burden of being your only friend. Do you remember when you were in high school and started dating, and you had a core of close friendships? If time, responsibilities, and a change in focus have made it difficult to maintain once cherished friendships, change your focus and your schedule, and make time for your friends. They can provide a valuable support system and help you keep a balanced perspective.

Relax

Quit worrying about outcomes. Be in the process, keep moving, and ask God—or the universe or whatever works for you—for what you want. Stop worrying about wanting more. Ask for more! Ask for big things and take action, and God will bring your desires and chance together. What some call luck, I just call God's answers. Be positive and don't get discouraged. Never give up! You will only fail if you stop trying. Never give up on yourself or God. What might look like an ending is sometimes just the beginning of something wonderful.

It's Up to You

I hope you realize there is no silver bullet. The choice is squarely on you. To recover your American Dream, you may need to change how you think, what you eat, and how you spend your time and with whom. It requires a lifestyle change and a mind-set shift.

Americans are used to a quick fix. I once told my doctor that I felt like an Indy car and he was the pit crew, implying "hurry up and keep me on the track!" A lifestyle and attitude change is not a pill you can take once and be cured. It means changing your habits and your way of thinking, and reframing old beliefs. Movement creates a mindshift almost immediately. Commitment and optimism are powerful forces that beat fear and pessimism every time. Have faith, take action, and transform your reality.

A personal, business, or mind-set coach can be an invaluable investment. Even those who are born with incredible ability and talent, including great athletes, need a coach. You can't expect to reach your full potential without someone to help you hold yourself accountable, and to listen, guide, and encourage you in fulfilling your dreams.

The Secret

When I was a broker trainer, the new recruits would always ask for the "magic bullet." They wanted to know the one thing that would make them successful. In business, as in life, there is no one thing. There is no secret! Success requires only desire, hard work, and discipline, in addition to a positive attitude, focus, and the ability to take action.

If there were just one factor that sits above all others, it would be the strength of your desire to achieve your goals. You hear of mothers who have single-handedly lifted a car to rescue their children. This is desire. Nothing deters someone who is this committed. If you want to make changes in your attitude, lifestyle, or career, your level of intention must be strong.

Anything you look at from the outside and covet—such as the lifestyle of a professional athlete, actor, or person who's successful in business, or someone else's wonderful marriage—takes hard work. These things don't just happen by magic. It takes consistent effort and focus where it counts. It takes the conscious act of avoiding avoidance and constantly striving to become better. People are happiest when they are growing, and this requires effort. So be happy and start creating growth.

I've never been the fastest starter, or the smartest, but I'm the most consistent. I just never give up. I know that everything doesn't have to be done in a day. The key is to keep going. I surround myself with books, articles, and even movies to keep myself inspired. I feed my mind good food, and it keeps my mind healthy, happy, and focused on the positive.

In order to achieve what you want in life, observe and imitate others who have accomplished what you desire. If someone else can do it, believe that you can, too. Never settle for self-imposed limits. I used to give the closing speech for financial advisors when they graduated after months of extensive training. I shared with them about what to expect in the real world and the keys to success. I asked them, "Who in this training can make 50 phone calls a day (everyday) for the next two to three years?"

Naturally, all 75 to 100 hands would go up. I told them that if they made this many calls, regardless of hang-ups, wrong numbers, and busy signals, they would achieve guaranteed success and make six figures. Smiles lit up their faces. Then I told them (based on my experience as a manager) that only one or two of them would do it, and I was right!

Why? Lack of discipline! Many people enter the brokerage world with dollar signs in their eyes, failing to realize their unrealistic expectations and poor work ethics put them in a situation that is a set-up for disappointment. Their ego resiliency is too weak to deal with the strain of the position. Their desire to avoid rejection will outweigh their desire to make six to seven figures.

My success has been totally dependent upon doing what others are *not* willing to do. In the beginning, as a fledgling financial advisor, I made 250 to 300 phone calls a day for over two years. Friends, faith, and fitness helped me keep pushing ahead.

Taking small strategic actions consistently over the long-term is more powerful than doing something tremendous once or for a short period of time.

The greatest coaches, athletes, and other successful people do the simple things great. Countless individuals might be smarter and better networked than you are, but you can create an advantage through consistent effort and willpower. What is your advantage? Focus on these elements while maintaining balance in all facets of your life.

Many people ask how I got to where I am and how I stay so fit and happy. Human beings have similar emotions. I don't like people hanging up on me; I prefer the taste of donuts over tofu; and getting up early to workout is tough, at times. Here are some tips that keep me disciplined and motivated:

- Mentally commit to the task or goal.

  Whether it's getting in shape, finding a better job, or staying engaged in your present career or relationship, you must want it! Forget your *need* for something and focus on *wanting* it. Write down your goal and sleep on it for a day or two. If you are still committed to the goal, then get busy.

- Act as if you have already attained your goal.

  Don't go out and spend a million dollars before you've earned it, but hold the attitude and feeling inside that having a million dollars will give you. If you think you'll feel more relaxed and secure, create those feelings in yourself right now. Keep inspiring pictures and motivational messages where you can see them frequently throughout the day.

- Have a plan of action and execute it.

  Follow through is always the hardest element of any plan. Create your plan for change and be sure to account for what it will take in terms of energy, time, and capital. For example, will you need different food, clothes, a change in your daily routine, or support from your spouse?

- Create accountability.

  Invite your spouse, friends, family, and especially a

coach to help you hold yourself accountable to your goals. You might work harder to avoid letting one of these people down than you would for yourself.

- Track your progress.

  Nothing measured, nothing changed! What gets measured gets done.

- Take small, consistent actions.

  This means take "baby steps." If you can only do a little on any given day or week, that's great. The key is to think about your goal daily. Visualize your goal as complete and the satisfaction you will feel. Thinking positively leads to positive results.

- Course correct.

  As you move forward, your plan will need adjusting to reflect the feedback you get when you take action. Expect it, and make changes when necessary.

- Never give up.

  You only fail when you stop trying! This is where faith, prayer, and discipline take over. Desire and faith will always win out. Unexpected resources will come your way when you persevere, but failure is guaranteed if you stop.

- Reward yourself along the way.

  Don't wait until you reach your goal. Celebrate the little victories to help you stay motivated. Finally, reward yourself when your goal is achieved.

Appreciation

I have come to realize, often too late, to appreciate things more. Like most people, I have taken many things for granted—my past career, the money I earned, friendships, my old dog, or relatives and family members that have passed. Yet, with each loss, I have learned to have greater appreciation for the things I have in the present. Tell the people you love how *much* you love them. A smile, a hug, or a kiss will make both of your lives better. A simple smile or hello will brighten the day of a co-worker or even a stranger on the street. Make time for the things in life that matter the most. Assess your life, what you want, need, and what will make you happy and excited.

Life is so simple, but it can also be cruel. If you are healthy, realize you already are a very wealthy person and be thankful for it. Learn to live in the moment and enjoy the present. Nothing else matters, because you cannot change the past or predict the future. Too much energy is wasted in ruminating over what already has taken place. Perfect the *now*. Keep your mind focused on the present with appreciation.

Have the Courage and Confidence to Pursue Big Dreams

Never fear failure but rather fear looking back with regret for never trying. A perfect example of this is a friend I met in college. His father's best friend planned to open a chain of stores that sold fast-food hamburgers. He thought the idea would never work. Who would buy a hamburger from a store called "McDonald's?"

In my own experience, in the early 1980s, my friend David Steinberg and I talked about opening a store in Chicago to sell Apple Computers. We decided the idea was too risky, and we were just getting on our feet at Merrill Lynch. To this day, we talk about the "what if?"

Camilo Villegas, a professional golfer, has an incredible workout regimen, and hanging on the wall in his gym is a sign emblazoned in block letters that serves as a reminder: "Sacrifice or Regrets…You Choose."

Living a Values-Based Life

I'm a firm believer in "Karma," (a Hindu word referring to the law of cause and effect). What goes around eventually comes around. Bad things happen to those who harm others. If you only care about yourself, you will eventually be alone. If you want love and happiness, you must be willing to give love and happiness. Be a giver of these things, not a taker.

We have become a selfish society. "Every man for himself" is often the motto, in and out of the workplace. In the office, I have seen many who have become masters of "managing up," which refers to neglecting to do what is right for the client and only doing what is politically correct or likely to further their own career. While it can be an effective self-preservation tool on Wall Street and in corporate America, it's detrimental to the clients, other employees, and to the culture of the organization.

Nothing comes easy. To earn over $100,000 per year takes a lot of work and effort. To earn more than this, the level of intelligence, hard work, and perseverance required goes up significantly. The key is to be thankful for what you have—and also for what others have—and be charitable to those less fortunate.

CHAPTER SEVEN

Success and Happiness

Success is not the key to happiness.
Happiness is the key to success.
If you love what you are doing,
you will be successful.

~ Albert Schweitzer, Nobel Peace Prize 1952

Most people strive for success and happiness, thinking that one follows the other. But is this true? Perhaps you began your career with a sense of ambition and excitement. Your new position, office, and title gave you the opportunity to acquire the success you always dreamed of, and you assumed this would make you happy. However, the time you put in and the excesses required of you to excel took on time-consuming momentum. As a result, happiness got left in the dust. More outward success brings on more responsibilities; it's a bigger "nut" you have to meet each month. Soon, the things you once wished for become burdens rather than assets. By putting your focus on success rather than happiness, it's like you will inadvertently create a life to which you feel enslaved rather than the freedom and joy you were expecting.

Let me illustrate this point by comparing the experiences that are possible when you focus on happiness versus success.

Focus on Success	Focus on Happiness
Struggle	Joy
Impatience to reach an ever-elusive destination	Enjoying the journey
Counting money	Watching sunsets
Future-focused	Being present
Strive for quantity/quality things	Create quality experiences

Focusing solely on success *or* happiness puts opposing forces to work. For example, when you strive for success, you are struggling to reach a destination, whether it's a certain position or net worth number. You imagine yourself enjoying your accomplishments and slowing down to watch the sunset at some point in the *future*, even as you tolerate the fact that you are *not* enjoying your experience in the present. Unfortunately, the future you imagined sometimes never arrives. If you don't know how to enjoy yourself now, having money and success won't teach you. More likely, you will decide the sunsets can wait until you achieve the *next* milestone of wealth, or you'll keep your head down and continue to drive forward in fear of losing what you've acquired.

You Can Have Both

The key I missed early in life was learning to recognize and control my thoughts and feelings. I had no direction or coaching to get through the challenges. I was afraid to seek help for fear of appearing weak. I felt as if everyone was looking to me, but I had no one to turn to for support. In youth, your body and brain chemistry have the resilience to allow you to compete and put in long hours. As you get older, your ability (and desire) to perform at this level wanes. In order to keep going and growing, you must learn to use your energy wisely.

In Chapter Four, I asked you to create a personal "Chart for Change." Now I'd like you to take it a few steps further and ask yourself some similar questions. If you'd like help with this, you can go to my website (www.michaelmarciniak. com) and download my free Goal Setting Form.

The Success-Focused Model

- What have you achieved so far?

- Where would you like to be?

- What is your estimated timeframe to get there?

- Is it reasonable?

- What are the likely obstacles you will face?

- What steps can you take to realize your goal?

The Happiness-Focused Model

- What motivates you to pursue a particular goal?

- Have you discussed it with your spouse or significant

other? Is your spouse behind this endeavor? How will your spouse support your efforts? What impact, if any, will it have on your family?

- Will reaching for or attaining your goal bring about any unintended consequences, such as moving, budgeting, or spending less time with the people you love? How will you manage these shifts?

- Are you happy? What issues are currently in the way of your happiness?

- What do you think achieving your goal will give you that you don't already have?

- What experience do you want that is presently lacking? Are you willing to acknowledge that you can have that experience right now?

Also write down the 10 things that are most likely to stop you from achieving your goal and any other perceived obstacles. Recognize what is good in your life right now. Once you have it all on paper, put it away for a day or two. Then take out your goal sheet again and decide if this is truly what you want. If the answer is "yes," you know your destination and you can set your course.

You need a sound plan of action to close the distance between where you are and where you want to be. Be realistic as well as ambitious. Too often, when we hear the word "success" we think of money, position, or title. If you want to have success and happiness, you need to reframe your thinking. Happiness goals are "being" goals. Being present allows you to enjoy the experience.

The path to happiness begins by realizing that money will not guarantee happiness. According to Phillip B. from www.lottobuster.com (2/22/10), 35 percent of all Big Lotto winners file for bankruptcy within 10 years of what should have been the greatest financial event of their lifetime. This statistic does not take into account the "winners" who went through divorce, drug and alcohol issues, and other problems. People who inherit wealth and entrepreneurs, who hit it big in a short period of time, often struggle with the unintended consequences of wealth; some lack the preparedness needed to manage their money wisely. Just when they thought they could kick back by the pool and enjoy life, they realize they have to decide where to put their money and how to spend it. They become encumbered with all the additional work that goes into maintaining a high-end lifestyle. In a *Washington Post* article, AOL founder James V. Kimsey observed, "Why it takes so many (nine) people to sustain me is hard to explain."

Being rich below the radar screen and anonymously financially independent is freeing. When your mega-wealth is publically known, you need to worry about security, management, and all the con artists who will try to rip you off. The point is that you can have all the money in the world, but will you be happy? Having wealth is a responsibility that carries its own set of problems. Money is only good if you have people to enjoy it with—and you are *prepared* to have it. You need good health to enjoy life, faith for inner peace, and values to help you to manage your money responsibly and allow others to respect and trust you. If your whole focus is success as a number, the journey will be miserable, and you will become worn down by the pressures you have created.

Growing up poor, I was on a mission to put myself in a position to make money. I worked long hours, ate a lot of high fat foods, and worked out only sporadically. My whole being was outward focused. In the background lingered thoughts and fears about what others were thinking of me, how I was perceived, and fear of failure in my career. I was haunted by questions such as: *When will I have enough?* and *How much is enough?* All I thought about was getting to the next step. My central focus was the job and all the baggage that came with it. Looking back, I should have reframed my thoughts and feelings from *how* and *when*—to *who, what, why* and *where*. Let's go through the success and happiness chart again and take a closer look.

Success Focus	Happiness Focus
How am I perceived? How am I doing? How can I get to the next level? How much am I making? How much is enough? How can I do more?	*Who* will enjoy my success with me? Who am I really? For whom am I doing all this? Who are my friends?
When will I retire? When will I get the next promotion? When will I have enough?	*What* do I really want? What makes me happy? What matters most? What are my priorities?
	Why am I doing this?
	Where do I find the most happiness?

Assessing my goals from the viewpoint of either success or happiness never dawned on me. I was so determined to keep my job. Should I have left the job sooner? Absolutely not! I needed to make money while I could. For me, I needed to satisfy my ambition to become financially independent. But a different perspective certainly would have made me appreciate life and my success more. I would have not taken so many wonderful acquaintances for granted. I would not have felt so entitled. I would have balanced my focus to include other areas of life that were more important than my career.

Had I done it right, I would have enjoyed the position *and* the journey. Like most things, you never appreciate them until they're gone. Being happy with what you have, living free of worry and anxiety, and laughing often like a child should be a part of everyone's American Dream. By giving the need for happiness more attention, your level of material success will also rise.

Career in the Balance

Achieving the American Dream that made this country great takes work. Life, liberty, and happiness come in exchange for providing value to others. The founders of our country rejected the model of an idle upper class and monarchy—which enjoyed inherited status and wealth—in favor of the promise that anyone who is *willing to work for it* can become as wealthy as their abilities and imagination will allow.

You need your job or career to support your family and home life, but you can't do much for your family if you are personally out of balance because you are working too much and are excessively committed to your career. No one ever said the American Dream was about working yourself to an early, lonely death!

A career is a marathon, not a sprint. When you work, you deserve to get paid. No less and no more than what you agreed to upon accepting the offer of employment. At the end of each pay period, you and the firm are even. If they provide benefits as part of your compensation, take them. If they provide two, three, or four weeks of vacation, take that, too. Don't be a martyr—vacations are a must.

No one at work will remember that you gave up your health or your family for the firm. As a manager, I had less respect for the people I supervised if they didn't take care of their own needs and the needs of their families. Perhaps your immediate supervisor feels the same way. You must recharge your battery. If you have your own company, it's up to you to give yourself a vacation on a regular schedule.

Working nonstop doesn't make you more effective. You must take time off—no matter how essential you are to the company. You can't help anyone else if you're exhausted.

The average American worker lives paycheck to paycheck, which is a tough way to go through life—it's definitely *not* the American Dream. It's harder if you don't like what you're doing and even worse if you can't take time off without losing your job. In this case, try taking mini-vacations throughout the day. As Dr. Loehr points out, mini-breaks only need to be a few minutes or even a few seconds.

These breaks should occur every 90 minutes or so. Turn your chair so that your back is to your desk and just close your eyes for a few seconds. Take a walk to get some water or give someone a compliment. Vacations and mini-breaks should be cherished and planned. Of course, there will be times when your boss, client, or patient needs you, or something else comes up unexpectedly. The point is that in an eight- to 12- hour workday there are always opportunities you can take to recharge your batteries.

Manage Your Thoughts

Nothing has greater influence over the direction of your career than your thoughts. They set the tone for the day and your expectations as to whether others will see you as capable. Your thoughts determine the limit of how far you will go and what it will take to get there. You can make it hard, or you can make it easy—it all comes down to your thoughts. It's amazing how the "little voice" of negativity, if left unchecked, can control your experience. When things are good, it creeps in to tell you that you don't deserve it, or it's too good to be true and something bad will happen soon. When things are bad, it will happily remind you how worthless you are and that you are doomed to ongoing failure and strife.

Misunderstood thoughts cause most of our problems. Old thought patterns reinforce beliefs, which many times are not true. Our thoughts are often fear-based. We fear that we won't have enough money, love, time, business, or health. This type of thinking can produce the very conditions we fear!

Take action to counter negative thoughts. Action will lead you out of fear and toward results. When you are busy being productive, there is no room for negative thoughts in your mind. True happiness and personal growth can occur only through improving the quality of an individual's thoughts.

Learn to manage that little voice inside. Try telling it: *Thank you for sharing* and then insert a positive affirming thought such as: *I am grateful for the many blessings in my life,* or *I welcome these challenges because they are preparing me for even greater success.*

Your moods will rise and fall with circumstances. Yet, you must be prepared to master them and take positive action to control your destiny.

> **Weak is he who permits his thoughts to control his actions; strong is he who forces his actions to control his thoughts.**
>
> **~ Og Mandino, Author of**
> **The Greatest Salesman in the World**

Be Indespensible

The best job security is to provide the most value to your company, but don't make the mistake of believing that working 80-plus hours per week is the only way to do it. You can add immeasurable value to your employer through brainpower, skill, and enthusiasm.

Continuing education will help you grow as a person and increase your skills. By proactively seeking more education, you show your employer that you are committed to increasing your competency. This puts you on the radar for promotion and career advancement.

Always have a forward-focused attitude. Attend all meetings and take copious notes. Demonstrate that you are engaged in the conversation and share well-thought-out, creative solutions with your team. You will stand out as a leader and winner, and you won't have to give up your entire life to do it.

Make it New

Mix it up. Change things around. Change your habits. Come to work at a different time and leave at a different time. Travel a new route to work and back. Switching out your desk set or pictures can make the whole office feel new and vibrant. Clean out your files and rearrange your desk or the furniture. If you have an opportunity to move to a better office, do it. If you need a bigger change, see if you can represent a different product line, change territories, or get a transfer.

Routine is nothing more than a rut. If there is little or no struggle, there will also be little success and joy. Lack of challenge is nothing more than trying to avoid fear or having lack of purpose. Demand more from yourself. Take some risk. Avoid playing it safe, and remember that you are in control.

After five years in the same position, I became bored, but I got a huge boost when I focused on reinventing my job position and myself. If you don't have that luxury, it will be even more important to focus on the things you *can* change.

Often the necessary change lies within you. Sometimes you just need to be present and treat every task as important, no matter how mundane or routine it might seem. You may have your own ideas as to how *you* can change to rid yourself of boredom. Have the courage to put your creative ideas into action, and your courage will be rewarded.

The New Year is a great time to explore making changes. It's the time to set budgets, plan for the upcoming year, and sit down with your boss or employees to set goals. Usually, they ask what you would like to accomplish. I typically state my intention to recreate myself in order to make the job fun and to bring it to the next level. Having a goal, a plan, and a way to measure results makes you accountable and helps you stay on course. Make sure your work goals are in line with the overall corporate goals *and* your personal goals. For example, consider attending speeches, put effort into building your team, or participate in out-of-the-office training events in order to strengthen your weakest area. Perhaps you need to improve your listening or presentation skills, or your ability to hold others accountable in a positive, non-confrontational manner. The key is to have fun and create growth that will make everything more exciting and less stressful.

Afterword

I have listened to numerous motivational speakers and read countless books on the importance of having a positive attitude. There is no one prescription for happiness, health, or freedom. Every U.S. citizen has the right to live the American Dream. The difference between people who achieve their goals and those who do not is about five inches. This is the approximate amount of space between your two ears!

Some speakers and books will resonate with you; others will leave you hanging and hoping. Timing and your willingness to accept the message determine whether the lesson is received. Are you ready to accept the message in this book? It's up to you. Change has to come from within. If you want happiness, you must be happy with yourself. Other people cannot do it for you. Even if they could, it would be only a temporary fix.

There's no single solution, and this is why I believe in balance. Everything has to work in harmony. I need strong faith, fitness to maintain my health and counteract stress, financial security to ward against emotional insecurity and worry, and a network of family and friends to enjoy it all with.

What do you need? Are you willing to change course and begin perfecting your American Dream? Life and the dream exist to be enjoyed. Don't feel guilty if you are already there. If you have reached your goals, then it's your job to help others achieve what you already have. If you are still striving toward achieving your dream, don't quit or give up hope just because it feels far away at times—and never feel guilty once you obtain it. Don't fear success. Relish it!

The purpose of living the dream is not only self-fulfillment and enjoyment, but also the ability to help others. Charity is the pinnacle of the American Dream. So, please don't forget those who are striving and in need of a boost. In the end, it's what's in your heart and soul, not what's in your wallet that counts.

I wish you a happy and prosperous journey.

Mike Marciniak

Resources

AUTHOR'S WEBSITE:
www.michaelmarciniak.com

Mike can be reached by phone at (941) 812-2219, or
e-mail him at Memconsultgroup@aol.com.

Books

Adams, James Truslow, *The Epic of America* (originally published by Boston, Little, Brown, and Co. in 1931; republished by Simons Publishers: Portland, Maine, 2001).
Mr. Adams coined the term "American Dream" in this book.

Carlson, Richard, *Don't Sweat the Small Stuff... and it's All Small Stuff* (This author has written a series of these books, published by Hyperion.)

Chandler, Steve. *Shift Your Mind, Shift the World* (Bandon, Oregon: Robert D. Reed Publishers, 2010).
This book contains eighty brief chapters on how to shift your mind to a positive frame. Chandler frames issues in a unique way to provide a different approach and get a fresh start.

Covey, Stephen, *The 7 Habits of Highly Effective People* (New York: St. Martin's Griffin, 1997).

Dungy, Tony, *Quiet Strength: The Principles, Practices, and Priorities of a Winning Life* (Carol Stream, Illinois: Tyndale Momentum, 2008).

Ferris, Timothy, *The Four-Hour Work Week: Escape 9-5, Live Anywhere, and Join the New Rich* (New York: Crown Archetype, 2009).
> Rarely do I ever read a book twice. I have read this one three times. It is loaded with provocative thoughts to get you to open to new ways to approach business and life. After you have read this book, you may be ready to leave your nine to five job!

Ford, Norman, *The Sleep Rx: 75 Proven Ways to Get a Good Night's Sleep* (New York: Prentice Hall, 1994).
> Ford covers every possible cause of poor sleep patterns and provides solutions to turn your night time into sleepy time.

Hendrix, Harville, *Getting the Love You Want: A Guide for Couples* (New York: Henry Holt & Co; Revised and Updated Edition, 2007).

Lehman, James, *The Total Transformation Program* (audio/CD) (Legacy Parenting Company, 2004).

Loehr, James E., *Stress for Success Jim Loehr's Program for Transforming Stress into Energy at Work* (New York: Random House, 1997).

Loehr, James E., *The Power of Full Engagement* (New York: Crown Business, 1998).
Dr. James E. Loehr is an inspirational speaker and true role model for me. He "walks the talk" in leading a balanced healthy, lifestyle. This book will help you transform stress into positive energy. I have been through many programs in my life. The Human Performance Institute, founded by Dr. Loehr, truly changed my life and how I approach life. This book will give you a sound footing to move forward in a positive, balanced way.

Maas, James B., *Power Sleep: The Revolutionary Program That Prepares Your Mind for Peak Performance* (New York: HarperCollins, 1998).
Dr. Maas's book explores the dynamics of sleep and why a sound night's rest is so beneficial to good health.

Mandino, Og, *The Greatest Salesman in the World* (New York: Bantam, 1983).

McGraw, Phillip C., *Relationship Rescue: A Seven-Step Strategy for Reconnecting with Your Partner* (New York: Hyperion, 2007).

Moeller, Kristen, *Waiting for Jack: Confessions of a Self-Help Junkie: How to Stop Waiting and Start Living Your Life* (New York: Morgan James Publishing, 2010).

Osteen, Joel. *It's Your Time: Activate Your Faith, Achieve Your Dreams, and Increase in God's Favor* (New York: Free Press, 2009).

Joel Osteen has a way of showing you the glass is always half full. Given the many issues you can encounter going through life's journey, he finds a way to stay optimistic through prayer, positive attitude and building a closer relationship with God.

Parker, Sam and Anderson, Mac, *212: The Extra Degree* (Naperville, Ilinois: Simple Truths, 2006). Also on DVD from New Legend Media (2008).

Ray, James Arthur, *Harmonic Wealth: The Secret of Attracting the Life You Want* (New York: Hyperion, 2009).

Stevens, Tom G., *You Can Choose To Be Happy: Rise Above Anxiety, Anger and Depression* (Palm Desert, CA: Wheeler-Sutton Publishing Co., 2010).

Articles

Matthew Warshauer 2003 article "Who Wants to be a Millionaire, Changing Conceptions of the American Dream" (*American Studies Today Online*, www.americansc.org.uk/Online/American_Dream.htm)

Adrian Savage, Author, Lifehack Management (www.Lifehack.org), 2007.

Bob Parsons, CEO and Founder of www.GoDaddy.com; "16 Rules for Success in Business and Life in General" (http://www.bobparsons.com)

Vacation Rentals

Vacation Rentals by Owner (VRBO®) http://www.VRBO. COM

This is the largest and most popular vacation rental site. VRBO specializes in "by owner" vacation rentals, homes, condos, and cabins.

Training

Human Performance Institute (HPI)

I am not on the payroll with HPI. My goal is to get you in the best physical and mental shape of your life. HPI will put a strong foundation under your structure. If interested, call 407-438-9911 or email *info@corporateathlete. com*. HPI is located at 9757 Lake Nona Road in Orlando, FL, 32827.

P90X

If HPI is not in your budget, for $120.00 you can buy a 12 DVDs workout series including a meal plan and calendar. Tony Horton does a fantastic job keeping you motivated. The only equipment needed is a mat, some dumbbells or workout bands and a chin up bar. You can do the entire program in your living room or bedroom. Take it slow with this program as you will feel muscles you never thought you had. Be sure you get permission from your doctor. Dial 800-461-1535 to speak to a P90X service rep.

The Total Transformation Program by James Lehman (Legacy Publishing Company, 2004.) Call 1-800-291-5028 or visit http://totaltransformation.com to order.

A step-by-step program for parents to understand and manage their teenager's behavior. Teaches strategies to bring parents into alignment with one another and present a united front with effective parenting strategies. The program costs approximately $350 and includes nine DVD's and a workbook. For an additional $49 a month, a parental support line is available.

TLC5 – The Life Coaching Connection
Created by Success Coach & Author, Barbie Hall Gummin.

Call 303-809-4555 or visit www.tlc5.com.

TLC5 offers an affordable, full-time solution to stimulate and reinforce your positive self–talk. Learn from specialized, expert coaches who will help you clarify and achieve what you want most in your personal and professional life. You can also visit the TLC5 Coach Directory and find a coach of your own. Cost is $100/YR or $15/MO for an individual. Group rates for businesses and organizations are also available.

About the Author

*The mind wants to continually dwell on the
past and worry about the future. Therefore, follow your
heart, which wants to enjoy the present.*

~ Mike Marciniak

Mike continues his quest for the ultimate American
Dream and is trying to impact as many lives as possible
through giving talks and his daily tweets, blogs, and books.

Mike "walks the walk and talks the talk" by clearly following the principles in this book. Since leaving Wall Street,
he has biked throughout Florida, Oregon, the Napa Valley,
Ireland, and France. He has traveled through Italy, Spain,
and England, and gone skiing in the Swiss Alps in Zermatt,
Switzerland. He cherishes his time with his family, and his
goal is to continue traveling the world to see the sights, and
to bike, ski, raft, and fish.

For the past three years, Mike has worked alongside
one of his long-time friends, David Steinberg. Although they
never opened that Apple Store, they have always envisioned
working together in some capacity. Mike's current position
is Director of Marketing for DLS Capital Management, a
boutique money management firm founded by David.

Mike has done coaching calls for TLC5, as well as
speeches for numerous philanthropic organizations. Begin-

ning in 2013, he will partner with Dennis Mosely-Williams and Tom Frisby, the founders of DMW Strategic Consulting (DMWSC), which creates custom marketing and practice management solutions for financial entrepreneurs across America. In this role, Mike will inspire, innovate, and accelerate lives and careers.

Mike supports various charities, but he is especially passionate about The House of Prayer in Bradenton, Florida, to which he contributes much needed clothing and food for the homeless.

Mike wants you to follow your dreams and heart, and would welcome an opportunity to touch your life in a positive way. To you and your family, he wishes health, wealth, and happiness.